ROCKIN' YOUR BUSINESS FINANCES

A STEP-BY-STEP WORKBOOK TO MAKING MORE BY MAKING LESS

CHRISTINE ODLE

Rockin' Your Business Finances:
A Step-by-Step Workbook to Making More by Making Less
© 2017 Christine Odle

Published by Rockin' Beeby Enterprises, LLC

ISBN: 978-0-9991351-0-5

VID: 20170729

Cover and Interior Layout by James Woosley, FreeAgentPress.com

Bumblebee logo hand drawn by Anna Woosley, AnnaWoosley.com

To my dear husband John.

I am who I am because of you.

CONTENTS

FOREWORD BY DAN MILLER

Ah yes, "If I were a rich man." That familiar plea from the popular movie, *Fiddler on the Roof*, seems to be the wish and the dream of many today. If only I were rich, then I wouldn't have to go to work every day. And yet, when we talk to those who are rich, getting out of working hard doesn't appear to be their goal at all. The money was not their primary goal. Rather, money showed up because the person wanted to do something worthwhile and thoroughly enjoyed the work they were doing.

Rockin' Your Business Finances is a fresh reminder that ending up wealthy is not a position reserved just for the lucky or those born into the right family. It is available for anyone—but may not come in the way portrayed in movies and fictional stories.

Responsible management of finances requires just as clear a plan as the business or career that created those abundant resources. Being good stewards of the wealth that explodes when we find our authentic fit in our work is not an automatic process. We must learn how to give, save, invest, and spend wisely. And yet I frequently see people who just assume the money will take care of itself. Or that money is just material—separate from the rest of our very real lives.

And thus, people end up with a fragmented life and frequently misuse the wealth with which they have been entrusted. Christine beautifully addresses this artificial separation and shows the way to a more fully integrated life. *Rockin' Your Business Finances* is a fresh approach to having not only a successful business, but an authentic and purposeful life.

As we move toward those dreams of happiness, meaning, fulfillment and riches, it seems reality assures us we will experience hardships along the way. It seems nature's way is for us to grow from the unexpected struggles that inevitably show up. But like the butterfly struggling to get out of the cocoon, our struggles are part of the process of making us fully alive. And like the butterfly, those struggles are not intended to limit or cripple us, but to allow us to develop our resilience, fortitude, compassion, personal excellence and wealth building wisdom.

We need a clear strategic plan to sow the growth of our businesses and lives that is directed and positive. The business people Christine profiles in this book describe that process over and over again. They did not avoid those struggles but found that having a clear plan revealed a light at the end of the tunnel.

You'll see that if you make great financial decisions you don't have to wait on someone to pick you for success. You pick yourself. If you blame, point fingers and make excuses, you'll block any chance for financial success. But you can open the floodgates by taking full responsibility for where you are, and can create the future you want, starting today.

Christine proposes real solutions and business models that are available to all of us. She offers the encouragement that there are opportunities that "fit" you—based on your unique goals and position.

I commend you on taking advantage of this intimate look inside the thinking, attitudes and practices of highly successful business owners. By modeling the behavior of those you are about to see in these pages and understanding your own "Four Walls," you too can put yourself firmly on the path from which there's no turning back—you be ***Rockin' Your Business Finances***.

Dan Miller

New York Times bestselling author of
48 Days to the Work You Love and *No More Mondays*

INTRODUCTION

Do you have a hobby, or a business? If you don't make a profit three out of five years, according to the IRS, it's a hobby. I was speaking at a conference, and an attendee came up afterwards and told me, "I love baking pies."

I said, "Awesome!"

"But I sell my pies."

"That's also awesome!"

"Well, am I a business?"

"That depends. Are you trying to make a profit selling your pies?"

"No, I just want to pay for my expenses."

Simply selling pies doesn't make it a business. Her intent is to only cover her costs, not to make a profit. She *could* set it up as a business, but it sounds like a hobby. She can make money with her hobby by selling her pies, but if she wants to create and run a business she needs to get out there and make a profit.

Will your love for your hobby survive it becoming your business? My hobby is photography. I love taking photos of wildlife, landscapes, rodeo, and car racing. I can take pictures all day long, but the second someone says, "I want to pay you for photos", I freeze. Don't pay me! I'll give it to you. It's a hobby. I tried to be a professional photographer, but within the first couple of opportunities of being paid, I suddenly hated my hobby. The first time I was paid to do a wedding, it was the worst wedding I'd ever photographed. The pictures were horrible. Photography, as a business, wasn't fun for me.

In *48 Days to the Work You Love*, Dan Miller writes about the meaning of vocation: "When there is an alignment of our skills, abilities, talents, personality traits and passions, we will recognize God's call. We will have found our sweet spot and will experience work that is fulfilling, meaningful, purposeful, and profitable." Ultimately if your vocation is a vacation, you've hit the sweet spot. But watch yourself and align yourself. If you decide you want to rent out kayaks, sea kayaks, paddle boards, and volleyballs, and you don't feel gypped that your customers are all out playing at the beach while you are stuck in your little box, go for it! If you love to ski, to teach others how to ski, and want to get paid doing it, go for it! But don't force your hobby into a business unless you really want a business.

Here is the Litmus Test for whether you have a hobby or a business: if, as you work your way through each chapter, you find yourself cringing at the thought of applying these principles, you have a hobby—and that's great, please put down this book and go have some fun with your hobby! If the principles resonate, you're in the sweet spot of making your vocation a vacation.

In the rest of this workbook, we are going to walk through ten different principles you can, and in my opinion, should, apply to your business to make it profitable. Thoughtfully used, these principles can help your business be *very* profitable. Whether you work in your business full or part-time, whether you hire contract employees, or have a full-time team, no matter if you are organized as an S Corp, DBA, Partnership, or an LLC, this book is for you. It is set up as a practical, hands-on workbook. After introducing a principle, I'll ask you to look at your specific business, think through how the principle applies, and then go apply it. The value in this book is in the application and the application will show you how to turn your hobby or business into an economic engine that will drive your income. So, grab a pen or pencil, quiet your mother's voice in your head telling you not to write in a book, and let's get started!

CHAPTER 1

BEING YOUR OWN BOSS

Why are you in business? Most business owners want to replace their paycheck, be their own boss, and make a decent living doing something that they're passionate about—or at least interested in. Unlike an employee who just must do the work, a business owner needs to market, sell, manage, and do a hundred other tasks indirectly related to the "actual work." Bookkeeping and business financial management are just two of those things.

Money is a huge source of stress for many business owners. Studies have shown that there are more heart attacks on Mondays than any other day of the week, and while the jury is out on the exact reasons, it is tempting to conclude that the stress of returning to the work week influences stress and the heart attack rate.

Regardless of whether you're a Sole Proprietor, a DBA, Partnership, an LLC, or an S Corporation, and whether you are part-time or full-time with your business, there is a very important mindset that allows you to become and stay more lucrative, allowing you to free up your time to concentrate on your business and to avoid the back-to-work Monday stress.

When you work for a company your highest goal is a promotion and/or raise. You are looking for a higher take-home pay. As a business owner, your focus is different. You're looking to bring in as much money as possible to the business—more clients, different clients, or better-paying clients. The focus isn't take home pay, it's dollars in the door. That works, but not in a vacuum. As a business owner, you need to have what I call a **tax mentality**. A tax mentality will allow you to make more by taking home less. I know it sounds weird, so let's break it down.

As an employee, you are taxed on your income in the form of federal tax, state tax (in most states), Social Security, Medicare taxes, and other deductions; after those are taken out you are left with your take-home pay. That take-home pay is what you have for your day-to-day expenses such as a computer, cell phone, car, and commuting expenses, in addition to regular living.

A business owner has the same taxes and many of the same expenses, but they don't have to pay themselves the same amount of money as a W2 employee to have the same or better quality of life since many of those expenses drive the business. Think of your business as a separate person. What does that person need to operate? Those expenses are legitimate business expenses and that money spent on those expenses are not subject to taxes because they are part of the expense of doing business. These items may be a computer, cell phone, car, and business travel.

JOURNEY TO A TAX MENTALITY...AND A DEBT FREE LIFE AND BUSINESS

As a little girl, I had a piggy bank. One of the things I loved to do was open the piggy bank, count the money, then put it back in the bank, and save up *more* money—nerd alert! I dreamed about teaching math and had even figured out a method of teaching math using money. When I grew up, I wanted to have a job in money. After college, my life plan was to work for a bank and live in a small town, and that's what I did for a few years. Eventually, I left banking and became a bookkeeper and office manager for a developer in Telluride, Colorado. I worked there for two years and loved the job! Then my employer decided to move the company to Denver and wanted me to move with it. He offered to significantly increase my salary, but I turned him down because I didn't want to live in a big city.

Being the great boss that he was, he asked me what I wanted to do instead. I told him I really loved doing what I did for him. So, he thought I should start my own company as a professional bookkeeper and office manager. The process of opening my own business came with new challenges—what to call my business, how to set it up, how would I be taxed, and who would I have as clients? He mentored me through the process and helped me learn, including the difference in mindset between an employee and a business owner. I went from being an employee working as a bookkeeper and office manager, to a business owner contracting out bookkeeping and office management. I didn't do everything right, but I learned along the way. The biggest and most important things I learned literally took me years to be proficient.

Having worked in banks, I had a debt mentality. Banks sell debt in the form of loans, credit cards, mortgages, and lines of credit, to name a few. When you take out a variety of debt, use the debt, and stay current on payments, you get a good credit score, mainly to buy more debt! After starting my own business, working with my husband and his family business, and running our personal lives, we operated with that philosophy. Using debt to build wealth, we bought property, assets, equipment, trucks, etc. We could make all our payments, so we just kept buying and building assets; all on credit. Then my husband saw this crazy, bald—headed guy on CNN in August 2001, Dave Ramsey, and came to me and said, "I don't know if you knew it or not, but I've been really scared about where our finances are. I really want you to go and learn what this guy knows." That's when I sat down and tallied up our debt and realized we were carrying debt of over *half a million dollars*!

Even though we were making good income as the self-employed, were keeping up with payments, and had great credit, all it would have taken was one rocky year and we would have lost everything. That's the scary, stressful thing about being self-employed, it doesn't take much to have one bad year. What a wake-up call! Half a million dollars...what had we been thinking?!

We got busy and very intentional. It took us seven and a half years to get everything paid off and just in time. In 2009, that rocky year came. We lost three big accounts, but because we had managed to become debt-free by that point, the only person we had to lay off was my husband!

ARE YOU BOB?

My business is no longer bookkeeping, it's business and financial coaching, and in that role, I see a lot of business owners like Bob, who runs a BBQ restaurant. Bob starts by saying, "I'm going to go under, I lost a big catering client, I'm in debt to my eyeballs, and I don't really understand what I'm doing financially. I don't know where the money goes and there never seems to be enough of it, even though my sales are typically very good and my customers rave about our food. If I go out of business my team will lose their jobs too, and many of them have families. I'm doomed if I do, and I'm doomed if I don't."

When I start to dig deeper I see many places for improvement. I find Bob is taking cash advances from his personal credit card for the business. His bookkeeper, who only comes in monthly, has no idea where money is coming from, because she enters transactions from the bank statements so all deposits are classified as income. At payroll Bob also gets a paycheck for wages; this is good because most business owners don't pay themselves. But then, Bob pays the credit card payments with his personal money. This is a problem because he loses out in the tax deduction of being able to expense the interest.

While all that doesn't sound so horrible, what is really happening is that the book-keeping is not accurate. A loan has been classified as income, then the company must pay Bob more to cover his rising personal expenses. Ultimately, he is probably paying much more in taxes than necessary and his numbers are not telling him what he really needs to know. All of this happened because he really doesn't understand the basic bookkeeping of his own business.

When digging even deeper, I ask him how his regular meetings with his bookkeeper go. He responds, "What meetings? I don't look at what she does, she just sends it all to the CPA." Same question, "How do those meetings with your CPA go?" Same answer,

"What meetings? The bookkeeper sends the information to the CPA, aren't they supposed to know what they are doing?"

Bob is putting too much in the hands of the bookkeeper and his CPA, and thus doesn't know if they are reporting correct figures or not. In his despair, he gets on edge and tries to blame them for not helping him enough in his business. But in reality, he is not helping them enough to know his real needs.

Bob hasn't been clear to the bookkeeper about what transactions are happening in the business and doesn't review the bookkeeper's work for accuracy. Bob has also hired a CPA, but rather than asking to be educated about his bookkeeping, he has said, "I need you to prepare my tax returns." The CPA is not working as an educator and doesn't know about the error in the income and expenses.

Bob is puzzled when I ask him about his personal finances. "I don't want to talk about my personal finances—I hired you for my business, Bob's BBQ." That's true, but if the business is to be successful, Bob needs to take home enough income to not implode his personal finances. Bob doesn't really know how much he takes home. Yes, he gets a payroll, but he also takes extra in unplanned draws, and by the time he gets that home it never seems to be enough.

Bob has the best BBQ joint in town, everyone loves Bob's BBQ, but his lack of financial savvy is sucking his time and energy, pulling away his focus, killing his love of his business, and making him crazy. It also has him on the edge of losing it all, and maybe closing his doors forever. Does this sound familiar?

LET'S GET STARTED – WHAT'S YOUR STORY?

Do you identify with any of Bob's story? How?

_____

_____

_____

_____

_____

Has Bob's story shifted your thinking? In what way?

_____

_____

_____

_____

_____

What is going well with your business's finances?

_____

_____

_____

_____

_____

_____

What is not going well with your business's finances?

_____

_____

_____

_____

_____

What do you hope to accomplish by reading this book?

_____

_____

_____

_____

_____

What is going well with your _personal_ finances?

_____

_____

_____

_____

_____

What is not going well with your *personal* finances?

_____

_____

_____

_____

_____

What questions about your business are popping into your head now?

_____

_____

_____

_____

_____

_____

_____

Hopefully we will be able to answer your questions in coming chapters. If not fill out the contact form at RockinYourBusinessFinances.com.

Let's Chat!

CHAPTER 2
INCOME AND EXPENSES

Almost 100% of the time, the biggest issue facing small business owners is not knowing what their sales will be. Unlike when they were employees and knew they were getting $*X,XXX.xx* on the 1st and 15th of the month, now they don't know if they'll make $100,000.00 this month or $0.00. I know the pain.

When I first started as a financial coach, some months I would get three new clients and other months I wouldn't get any. In the months without new clients, my personal and business month-to-month expenses continued while my income was flat.

This wild fluctuation is even more difficult for non-service-based businesses, like retail. December can be a huge month and January non-existent. Understanding the cycles in your industry will help you to manage your big income months properly so your smaller income months won't cause you to run out of cash. Lack of cash, typically, means debt begins to pile until the debt becomes crushing, you are out of money, and out of business.

Effective income and expense planning allows you to capture enough of the money in good times to flow over and support your business in the slower months to give you a runway. Your runway is how long you can pay for the things your business absolutely requires while you work to bring in income.

It's like how much time an airplane has to get off the ground—the more the better. A long runway allows you time to sell your products or services. A short runway is dangerous and means you need to hustle hard. No matter its length, having a good understanding of exactly how much time you have to make your business a success is imperative.

Be careful of the mindset that says, "I can't get a handle on the money in my business because the income is irregular income." It is a death sentence for your business. Irregular income won't kill you; every business faces it. What will kill you is ignoring it or throwing your hands up and acting like there's nothing that can be done about it.

THE FOUR WALLS

The easiest and best way to plan your runway is to identify the Four Walls in your business. This is actually a personal financial coaching concept brought over to help business owners. In personal finance the Four Walls make up your home. Without even one of those walls life as you know it could fall down around you. In your personal budget, the Four Walls are the same for everyone, in this order: Food, Housing, Transportation, and Clothing. We need something to eat, somewhere to live, a way to get to work, and clothes so we don't run around naked.

We can use those same Four Walls in our business. What are the things without which would be the functional equivalent of being naked in your business? Not every business has the same Four Walls, so it's a little more challenging, but once you have identified your Four Walls they operate exactly the same. Identify and hold the funding of the Four Walls sacred. Take care of first things first in your business.

The Four Walls of your business might be:

- Payroll

- Taxes—sales tax and/or payroll tax

- Inventory

- Office space and utilities

- Insurance—liability, worker's compensation

- Transportation—trucks, repairs, fuel, vehicle insurance

When you know your Four Walls, you know your runway. At any point in time you can compare the cash you have to what you absolutely need to keep your business open.

WHAT ARE YOUR FOUR WALLS?

1. _____

2. _____

3. _____

4. _____

BOB'S BBQ JOINT

Let's look at Bob's Barbecue Joint's Four Walls:

1. **Restaurant Location / Building**

2. **Payroll / Payroll Tax**

3. **Food**

4. **Utilities**

Without any one of those things, Bob's BBQ Joint closes. Without a location, there's nowhere for patrons to eat. Without payroll, there's no one to serve and cook for the customers. Without food, there's nothing to eat. And without utilities, the lights and kitchen equipment won't turn on.

Bob's best months are in the summer when the corn is sweet and his outdoor patio is full of happy families. He also does a brisk business during the holidays when local businesses throw big barbecue bashes. Bob should be planning his cash flow to cover his Four Walls when business is slow in January, February, and March and again in October and November. It's a big stretch to plan for January through March, and that is part of where we are able to identify some of his cash flow issues.

CHASING BACKWARDS

Your Four Walls will also help you stop chasing your expenses backwards. Chasing backwards is using this month's income to pay for last month's expenses. You are literally waiting for the check to come in and clear before you can send out your pretty, white envelopes. Not only is that method inefficient, it's stressful. If one key client or account pays slowly, the house of cards comes crashing down. Last month's income should cover this month's expenses. You don't have to hold invoices, bills, or checks when the income you're using to pay them has already arrived.

In the case of Bob's BBQ Joint, Bob needs to be planning that his huge catering month of December is able to cover most of his expenses for January, February, and March. When looking at the big picture, a best practice for Bob would be to look at last year's busiest months and build his budget for the entire year based on the best seven months' income. Then, leave himself a cushion in his accounts to cover, at a minimum, the Four Walls of those slower months.

THE TRIED AND TRUE BUDGET (SMILE WHEN YOU SAY THIS)

The best way to know your numbers is that tried and true method, writing it down. At the end of this chapter is a sample budget to get you started. You will notice the Four Walls are identified as well as some blank lines for you to fill in specific to your business. For now, don't worry about the timing of how cash flows through your business—we'll get into that in the next chapter. Just write down what you expect in terms of income and expenses for each month, considering seasonal variations. If you have trouble starting with this year, start today with THIS month. What does the month you are in right now look like? Not the perfect month, this month, then start next month.

Monthly Regular expenses are the same every single month. The Non-Regular column is for expenses that don't come monthly, like insurance, equipment repairs, business conference travel, etc. If you're paying $1,200 twice a year in car insurance for business, that $1,200 goes into the Non-Regular column. You may have several of those annual expenses. Bob's BBQ Joint pays $1,830 in workers' compensation insurance each August. That's a big bill and one of their Four Walls. We want to know that it is coming and plan for it.

In the next chapter, we'll talk about Sinking Funds, a method that will help you avoid a scramble when those Non-Monthly expenses come around.

VARIABLE EXPENSES

Variable expenses are those that don't happen monthly and are not as predictable as Non-Regular expenses, like insurance. For example, the amount of inventory you purchase will be in direct relation to demand and may be tough to predict very far in advance, especially if you're a new business.

Another example is a franchise fee. When you don't know how much you're going to sell, you don't know the amount of the franchise fee. Within your Four Walls, some expenses will be fixed and some will be variable, and you'll have to make an educated guess and modify as you go along.

It is very difficult to write in consistent, accurate monthly numbers over the course of the year without solid history. And, even then, this year might not look anything like last year. This is an excellent reason to always do your budget monthly, as each month is different. You are not trying to create a "perfect" month or an "average" month; you should be focusing on what happened this month and then plan next month accordingly.

WHERE TO GET YOUR NUMBERS

If you're a new business, you're going to be making an educated guess on both the income and expense side, and make frequent adjustments as you know more. If you're a more established business, you can look to history, but be careful because things change. Payroll changes, insurance costs change, everything changes. To become great at budgeting in your business, being proactive is key. Do a budget each and every month. Looking backwards is helpful, but it's not the end of the discussion. Don't fix it and forget it.

COST OF GOODS SOLD

If you manufacture or sell physical products, you must understand the difference between expenses and cost of goods sold. Expenses are things often labeled "overhead" while cost of goods sold are the expenses you incur to send a widget out the door. If you manufacture woven baskets, then your cost of goods sold includes your materials for each basket and your labor to create the basket. Keep careful track of how much it costs you to produce or purchase a widget because it will tell you how much you need to charge for it.

Cost of Goods Sold immediately brings up the issue of inventory, one of the most vexing issues for any manufacturer or reseller. While it is an important topic we only touch on it in this book. A good rule of thumb is to include your labor costs (payroll) as a COGS or at least list Labor *before* Expense "A" as it is typically a huge part of COGS and how you will calculate your margins and pricing.

THAT'S NOT INCOME!

One of the common places that unintentionally trips up business owners is mistakenly counting money into the business as income. It sounds crazy to think money coming in to your business may not be income, but it's a very important distinction that will save you money and confusion. When you put your personal money into the company that is not income. If you borrow from the bank to put cash into the business, that is not income. Those amounts will show on your Balance Sheet (see

Chapter 4), but they are not income. The big reason this distinction is important is because you don't want to pay tax on this money. When you lend money to the business, you've gone out, earned that money, and paid taxes on it already. If you bring it into the business as income, you will get to pay tax on it all over again.

I've seen this scenario happen with smart, sophisticated clients. It's a bookkeeping oversight that comes with a big penalty—double taxation. Any time money comes into the business, it's very important to determine exactly how to categorize that money. Is it income, money earned from doing business, a loan, or a capital contribution, i.e., you putting personal money into the business as equity, or perhaps you received a grant?

YOU'VE GOT THIS

The things discussed in this chapter highlight the difference between a hobby and a business. A hobbyist just wants to cover costs and have a little fun, a business owner digs into the meaty questions of income and expense knowing it will pay off in a thriving, financially successful business.

BOB'S BBQ, LLC
Profit/Loss Budget vs. Actual

	Actual	Budget	$ Over/Under
INCOME			
Food Truck Income			
Catering	$ 33,463.39	$ 60,000.00	$ 26,536.61
Special Events	$ 12,543.50	$ 10,000.00	$ (2,543.50)
Festivals	$ 3,500.00	$ 5,000.00	$ 1,500.00
Other Income	$ -	$ -	$ -
Other Income	$ -	$ -	$ -
Total Food Truck Income	**$ 49,506.89**	**$ 75,000.00**	**$ 25,493.11**
Restaurant Income			
Beverages	$ 7,514.95	$ 10,000.00	$ 2,485.05
Kids/Senior Meals	$ 9,918.39	$ 15,000.00	$ 5,081.61
Military Meals	$ 5,141.30	$ 2,000.00	$ (3,141.30)
Regular Meals	$ 68,591.50	$ 85,000.00	$ 16,408.50
To Go Orders	$ 25,928.77	$ 20,000.00	$ (5,928.77)
Total Restaurant Income	**$ 117,094.91**	**$ 132,000.00**	**$ 14,905.09**
TOTAL INCOME	**$ 166,601.80**	**$ 207,000.00**	**$ 40,398.20**
COST OF GOODS SOLD (COGS)			
Cost of Goods Sold			
Delivery Fee	$ 175.00	$ 200.00	$ 25.00
* Food Costs	$ 74,970.81	$ 62,100.00	$ (12,870.81)
Other COGS	$ -	$ -	$ -
Total Cost of Goods Sold	**$ 75,145.81**	**$ 62,300.00**	**$ (12,845.81)**
TOTAL COGS	**$ 75,145.81**	**$ 62,300.00**	**$ (12,845.81)**
GROSS PROFIT	**$ 91,455.99**	**$ 144,700.00**	**$ 53,244.01**
EXPENSES			
Payroll Expenses			
Bookkeeper	$ 10,000.00	$ 6,000.00	$ (4,000.00)
* Kitchen Staff	$ 45,200.00	$ 85,000.00	$ 39,800.00
* Wait Staff	$ 20,043.15	$ 20,000.00	$ (43.15)
Owner/Manager	$ 10,000.00	$ 10,000.00	$ -
Total Payroll	**$ 85,243.15**	**$ 121,000.00**	**$ 35,756.85**

Automobile						
Fuel	$	982.68	$	800.00	$	(182.68)
Insurance	$	427.62	$	200.00	$	(227.62)
Maintenance & Repairs	$	254.50	$	100.00	$	(154.50)
Other	$	-	$	-	$	-
Total Automobile	**$**	**1,664.80**	**$**	**1,100.00**	**$**	**(564.80)**
Depreciation						
Truck	$	575.00	$	300.00	$	(275.00)
Kitchen Equipment	$	-	$	275.00	$	275.00
Other	$	-	$	-	$	-
Total Depreciation	**$**	**575.00**	**$**	**575.00**	**$**	**-**
Insurance						
Liability	$	1,005.00	$	83.75	$	(921.25)
* Worker's Comp	$	1,830.00	$	152.50	$	(1,677.50)
Other	$	-	$	-	$	-
Total Insurance	**$**	**2,835.00**	**$**	**236.25**	**$**	**(2,598.75)**
Operating Expenses						
Bank Service Charges	$	303.00	$	120.00	$	(183.00)
Equipment Repairs	$	1,278.90	$	1,000.00	$	(278.90)
Interest Expense	$	3,854.13	$	2,500.00	$	(1,354.13)
Office Supplies	$	295.87	$	300.00	$	4.13
Professional Legal/Acctg	$	375.00	$	375.00	$	-
Rent	$	2,400.00	$	2,400.00	$	-
Total Operating Expenses	**$**	**8,506.90**	**$**	**6,695.00**	**$**	**(1,811.90)**
Utilities						
* Gas and Electric	$	1,614.95	$	1,700.00	$	(85.05)
Telephone	$	684.86	$	700.00	$	(15.14)
* Water	$	446.23	$	500.00	$	(53.77)
Debt Payments ($975 extra)	$	1,500.00	$	1,500.00	$	-
Total Utilities	**$**	**4,246.04**	**$**	**4,400.00**	**$**	**(153.96)**
TOTAL EXPENSES	**$**	**103,070.89**	**$**	**134,006.25**	**$**	**30,627.44**
NET INCOME	**$**	**(11,614.90)**	**$**	**10,693.75**	**$**	**22,616.57**

* The Four Walls

Profit/Loss Budget vs. Actual

	Actual		Budget		$ Over/Under	
INCOME						
Income A						
1)	$	-	$	-	$	-
2)	$	-	$	-	$	-
3)	$	-	$	-	$	-
4)	$	-	$	-	$	-
5)	$	-	$	-	$	-
Total Income A	$	-	$	-	$	-
Income B						
1)	$	-	$	-	$	-
2)	$	-	$	-	$	-
3)	$	-	$	-	$	-
4)	$	-	$	-	$	-
5)	$	-	$	-	$	-
Total Income B	$	-	$	-	$	-
TOTAL INCOME	$	-	$	-	$	-
COST OF GOODS SOLD (COGS)						
Cost of Goods Sold						
1)	$	-	$	-	$	-
2)	$	-	$	-	$	-
3)	$	-	$	-	$	-
Total Cost of Goods Sold	$	-	$	-	$	-
TOTAL COGS	$	-	$	-	$	-
GROSS PROFIT	$	-	$	-	$	-
EXPENSES						
Payroll Expenses						
1)	$	-	$	-	$	-
2)	$	-	$	-	$	-
3)	$	-	$	-	$	-
4)	$	-	$	-	$	-
Total Payroll	$	-	$	-	$	-

Expense A

1)	$	-	$	-	$	-
2)	$	-	$	-	$	-
3)	$	-	$	-	$	-
4)	$	-	$	-	$	-
Total Expense A	**$**	**-**	**$**	**-**	**$**	**-**

Expense B

1)	$	-	$	-	$	-
2)	$	-	$	-	$	-
3)	$	-	$	-	$	-
Total Expense B	**$**	**-**	**$**	**-**	**$**	**-**

Expense C

1)	$	-	$	-	$	-
2)	$	-	$	-	$	-
3)	$	-	$	-	$	-
Total Expense C	**$**	**-**	**$**	**-**	**$**	**-**

Operating Expenses

1)	$	-	$	-	$	-
2)	$	-	$	-	$	-
3)	$	-	$	-	$	-
4)	$	-	$	-	$	-
5)	$	-	$	-	$	-
6)	$	-	$	-	$	-
Total Operating Expenses	**$**	**-**	**$**	**-**	**$**	**-**

Utilities

1)	$	-	$	-	$	-
2)	$	-	$	-	$	-
3)	$	-	$	-	$	-
4)	$	-	$	-	$	-
Total Utilities	**$**	**-**	**$**	**-**	**$**	**-**

TOTAL EXPENSES	**$**	**-**	**$**	**-**	**$**	**-**
NET INCOME	**$**	**-**	**$**	**-**	**$**	**-**

* *The Four Walls*

IT'S YOUR TURN

Next to Bob's numbers try penciling in your own on the example or the blank form that follows. Additionally, all of the forms are available for download at RockinYourBusinessFinances.com.

_____

_____

_____

_____

_____

When thinking of your Four Walls, was it difficult to narrow it down to just four?

_____

_____

_____

_____

How does identifying the Four Walls of your business change how you use and save the income that comes through your business?

_____

_____

_____

_____

How difficult was it to complete the Income and Expense tables? Did you already have this in a program such as FreshBooks or QuickBooks?

_____

_____

_____

_____

_____

What other information do you need?

_____

_____

_____

_____

_____

In your mind, what is missing? Where do you need the most help?

_____

_____

_____

_____

_____

For FREE Spreadsheets and Forms,
visit RockinYourBusinessFinances.com.

CHAPTER 3
CASH FLOW

Your Profit/Loss Statement (P/L) says you made a profit, but your account is in the negative. Where's the money? You're charging more for your services than you made as an employee, but you still don't have enough to pay yourself as a business owner. Does this sound familiar?

This is cash flow, and you need to understand and plan for it. The fancy term is *Cash Flow Forecasting*, and, put simply, it's the amount of money you need to bring into your business so you can pay the things you need to pay, when you need to pay them, and have a profit or a positive cash balance at the other end. Cash flow is literally how the cash flows in and out of your business. Ninety percent of businesses are scrambling for cash. That's called *not* planning for cash flow!

In our last chapter, we talked about income and expenses. Cash flow isn't the same as your Profit/Loss Statement. Cash flow looks totally different, as it includes money you bring into the business and money you pay out of the business that are seen on both the Profit/Loss Statement AND the Balance Sheet (loan payments, asset purchases, credit card payments or draws). Money might flow into your business because of sales. Perhaps it flows in because you've personally funded the bank account to keep going. Maybe you transferred money from savings (Sinking Fund) into checking. No matter how it gets there, you want to be sure you can see where it is coming from, and where it is going out.

BANKING MATTERS

I advise clients to have three different accounts for each business.

"Wait a minute," a client exclaims, "I have four different businesses. You want me to have TWELVE different accounts?"

Yes, you want three accounts for each business because each one does something different for you. It's a lot to manage, but if you're very specific and intentional, you'll find it will help you immensely—a small price to pay to never scramble again.

The **Business Checking Account** is your day-to-day account, I call this the Operating account. All money coming into the business goes into this account, no matter the source, to be distributed appropriately. Transactions all come out of this account including paying your team, vendors, and bills, and then transfers to other accounts.

The **Business Emergency Fund Account** holds the money set aside for unexpected events and emergencies. Planning for emergencies is key, the amount in this account should be roughly three to six months of your general operating expenses, including your Four Walls, depending on your business. To figure out how much you need, you'll start with your Four Walls as described in the prior chapter. Then, add additional operating expenses. You want to have this money in case of unforeseen events. If your building burns down and you can't make widgets, will you want to keep your employees on payroll or give them severance pay so they can survive on something while looking for another job. If so, money to cover that expense should be in this account because the only other way to do that is to go into debt. When you spend money out of this account, it is a high priority to build it back up to that three to six-month amount.

The **Business Short-Term Funding Account** (or *Sinking Fund*) is for the big items you know or suspect are coming, the annual insurance payment, Christmas bonuses, a new product that you want to develop, or some cash for when you want to do something new and big. You might want to put your sales and payroll taxes here especially if they are due quarterly to keep you from spending it elsewhere. This is also where you save up for those smaller income months, because we know they are coming.

If you're good at keeping them separate, the three accounts can be at the same bank; however, if you're someone who sees the short-term funding account as a sort of back-up slush fund, I'd advise moving it to another bank.

Online banks, like Ally Bank and Capital One 360, not only have rates which beat a regular savings account rate, it takes two days to pull money out and that few days can help you think things through without panic. If you find that, whoops, we had a huge month in December, but January is going to have a cash shortfall and you'll need some cash for payroll on the 15th, you can plan for the two days and pull it out on the 12th or 13th.

I don't recommend overdraft protection. It's a form of debt and it gets used as a cash source trend as opposed to planning cash flow. Overdraft protection makes for lazy cash flow planning and racks up very quickly. And, it seems to be the hardest debt to pay off as a symptom of poor planning.

THE FOUR WALLS & CASH FLOW

Your Four Walls hold up your business, so every time your money comes in, you want to go down the list and pay those items first. If you have rent as one of your walls, pay the rent before anything else. If you cannot run your business without your employees, pay your payroll first.

One thing that should never be one of your walls is credit card payments. Nothing will take you backwards quicker than paying credit card debt first, especially before you pay your Four Walls expenses. The reason people do that is so they will be able to continue to use debt to pay bills in the future-that's just ineffective, cyclical cash flow planning. Going into debt to pay bills with credit cards is a cycle you need to unplug.

THE MONEY COMES IN...

Cash flow depends on the money coming in at a rate and in a quantity, that make the business viable. A very basic need of any business, but especially a small business, is to price services or goods correctly. It sounds painfully obvious that you need to price your services or goods to allow for a profit, but as obvious as it sounds, it is very common to underprice.

Many moons ago, I made $30,000 a year working as a bookkeeper, which works out to $15 an hour. When I started my business, I gave myself a raise to $16 an hour. Of course, that didn't work, so I charged $20 and had a goal of making $200 a day. I set myself up for consistent 10 hour days! Surprisingly, it still didn't work. Without an understanding of cash flow, it's impossible to know what to charge and you only realize your mistake after you've paid the business expenses and don't have enough left to pay yourself.

That's the origin of the classic lament, "I'm not taking a salary, because the business gets it all. And, I put all my money back into my business." Ultimately in a serviced-based business, you'll almost always need to charge at least double, sometimes triple what you want to bring home as a paycheck.

WHEN IT COMES

Cash flow is pinned on *when* the money is coming in. At Bob's BBQ Joint, when he caters a party he might contract for 50% of the meal to buy food and pay employees for prep & set up. The other ½ is due after the party is over. The timing on the booking, the party, and the final payment could be months in time. So, planning that cash is vital in making sure you cover your costs and make a profit. Planning your cash flow means understanding when your money is coming in, and how long of a runway that money should cover. It means you plan ahead for big and small expenses. You plan carefully for the ebb and flow of income.

Some people budget well over several months, but your cash flow might be better served by negotiating a contract that pays you each month. This could help your cash flow *and* your client's cash flow.

THAT IT ACTUALLY COMES

Another important factor is your receivables. Be assertive in collecting on your receivables. Those who work selling to the government in my neck of the woods have a very difficult time with this. The government may go six months before they send payment, and in the meantime, the business has a risk factor of going into debt paying their own suppliers. It's crazy, we don't go grocery shopping and expect the store to let us pay six months later!

Establish the non-negotiable parameters of your bills: 15 or 30 days from receipt, with a 21% late fee, or other agreement made at the time of the billing. Train your clients to pay by being the squeaky wheel. Call up and ask for it, there's no shame there. If you provide a good or service, it's reasonable to get paid for that good or service.

Once you know *what* you're charging, and *when* the money should be coming in, you match that with when you pay your bills--and not by chasing your expenses backward. Pay your March bills with February's money as opposed to trying to pay March's bills with April's money. It keeps you a step ahead and saves you many gray hairs.

With a properly planned cash flow you will be light years ahead of your business competitors and able to lay your head down on the pillow at night and sleep soundly.

BOB'S BBQ, LLC
Cash Flow

	Bank Acct/ Cash	Receivable/ Catering	Cash Sales/ Restaurant	Payables	Projected Balance
Beginning Balance	$ 5,300.00	$ -	$ -	$ -	$ 5,300.00
Week 1	$ 5,300.00	$ 10,000.00	$ 5,000.00	$ (5,000.00)	$ 15,300.00
Week 2	$ 15,300.00	$ 5,000.00	$ 5,000.00	$ (9,000.00)	$ 16,300.00
Week 3	$ 16,300.00	$ 2,500.00	$ 5,000.00	$ (11,000.00)	$ 12,800.00
Week 4	$ 12,800.00	$ 500.00	$ 6,500.00	$ (6,000.00)	$ 13,800.00
Week 5	$ 13,800.00	$ -	$ 5,000.00	$ (2,500.00)	$ 16,300.00
Week 6	$ 16,300.00	$ 500.00	$ 5,000.00	$ (1,500.00)	$ 20,300.00
Week 7	$ 20,300.00	$ 500.00	$ 5,000.00	$ (1,500.00)	$ 24,300.00
Week 8	$ 24,300.00	$ -	$ 2,500.00	$ (3,000.00)	$ 23,800.00
Week 9	$ 23,800.00	$ 250.00	$ 2,500.00	$ (5,000.00)	$ 21,550.00
Week 10	$ 21,550.00	$ -	$ 2,500.00	$ (3,000.00)	$ 21,050.00
Week 11	$ 21,050.00	$ -	$ 2,500.00	$ (5,000.00)	$ 18,550.00
Week 12	$ 18,550.00	$ 250.00	$ 2,500.00	$ (5,000.00)	$ 16,300.00
Week 13	$ 16,300.00	$ -	$ 2,500.00	$ (5,000.00)	$ 13,800.00
Week 14	$ 13,800.00	$ -	$ 2,500.00	$ (5,000.00)	$ 11,300.00
1st Quarter		$ 19,500.00	$ 54,000.00	$ (67,500.00)	

ENDING BALANCE $ 11,300.00

Cash Flow

	Bank Acct/ Cash	Receivable/ Catering	Cash Sales/ Restaurant	Payables	Projected Balance
Beginning Balance	$ -	$ -	$ -	$ -	$ -
Week 1	$ -	$ -	$ -	$ -	$ -
Week 2	$ -	$ -	$ -	$ -	$ -
Week 3	$ -	$ -	$ -	$ -	$ -
Week 4	$ -	$ -	$ -	$ -	$ -
Week 5	$ -	$ -	$ -	$ -	$ -
Week 6	$ -	$ -	$ -	$ -	$ -
Week 7	$ -	$ -	$ -	$ -	$ -
Week 8	$ -	$ -	$ -	$ -	$ -
Week 9	$ -	$ -	$ -	$ -	$ -
Week 10	$ -	$ -	$ -	$ -	$ -
Week 11	$ -	$ -	$ -	$ -	$ -
Week 12	$ -	$ -	$ -	$ -	$ -
Week 13	$ -	$ -	$ -	$ -	$ -
Week 14	$ -	$ -	$ -	$ -	$ -
1st Quarter		$ -	$ -	$ -	
ENDING BALANCE	$ -				

IT'S YOUR TURN

What have been your experiences in the past dealing with cash flow, both positive and negative?

_____

_____

_____

_____

_____

What seasonality affects your business?

_____

_____

_____

_____

_____

What elements of cash flow do you need a better handle on?

_____

_____

_____

_____

_____

How will you use the Four Walls of your business to plan cash flow?

_____

_____

_____

_____

Do you have a strong process for collecting and identifying receivables?

_____

_____

_____

How difficult was it to complete the Cash Flow table?

_____

_____

_____

What other information do you need? How and when will you get it?

_____

_____

_____

_____

For FREE Spreadsheets and Forms,
visit RockinYourBusinessFinances.com.

CHAPTER 4
FINANCIAL REPORTS

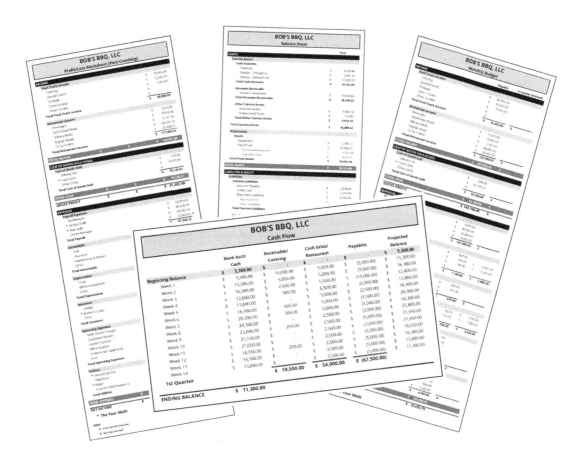

DO YOU KNOW YOUR NUMBERS?

There are a lot of shows about businesses on television these days: *Shark Tank*, *The Profit*, *Restaurant Impossible*, and many more.

Multi-millionaire experts ride in to save the day, and, about 80% of the time, one of the first things these experts discover is that the owners don't know their numbers.

If you watch any of *The Profit* shows, every single one of Marcus Lemonis' business cases are virtually clueless on what their numbers are telling them. They might know their margins—how much they sell something for, and how much it costs them —but that's about it. It's not enough to just know your margins.

They understand how the money comes into the business, but don't really understand how the money flows through the business. How do you figure out if that $150,000 piece of equipment is actually a good buy for your business or not? How do you analyze your business to know what to spend? How do you cut costs when not necessary or increase costs to make that return into bigger profits?

In some cases, they may not know what their labor costs them. With their share of Social Security, Medicare, workers' comp, unemployment benefits, any other benefits, and then paid time off, you can generally count on labor expenses being at least double of what you actually pay an employee. If you don't charge for any or all of those things to get it back in income, it must come out of your margins. So, margins are very important!

What do you need to know to make sure everything is included in your margins? Your numbers will tell you. Let's get down to what you need to understand for your business so you won't find yourself on *The Profit*!

MAKING A STATEMENT

You typically need four different documents to understand what your numbers are telling you and what they mean.

1) CASH FLOW STATEMENT

The flow of money (see Chapter 3)

2) PROFIT/LOSS STATEMENT

Income less Cost of Goods Sold less Expenses

3) THE BUDGET

Telling the money what to do (see Chapter 2)

4) BALANCE SHEET

Assets Owned less Liabilities Owed = Business Equity

Here's how to make those documents work for you. I always recommend that you complete your data entry, accounts balanced, and payroll taxes for last month by the 15th of the current month. That will give you time to analyze and plan for the coming month.

Reconciling your numbers by the 15th means that you'll have double checked your sales and the sales tax numbers, your payroll, and you'll be ready for the government payments that come due, usually, by the 15th. After all accounts have been reconciled (including Petty Cash & Credit Card Statements) and you've finished all reporting, then that gives you another two weeks in the month to really analyze and work with your numbers.

If you're a small company, just starting out, or you're not very big yet, getting these processes in place will help you to grow intentionally. If you are already off and running your business then getting this process in place will make your monthly forecasting much easier. When you are very specific about reporting your sales months, then you can start forecasting for next year—big companies forecast for the next 12 months and the next 5 years.

BUSINESS IS BUSINESS; PERSONAL IS PERSONAL

Another important concept is to **keep yourself and your business separate**. You have your own money, and your business has its own money. You may need to invest some of your personal money into the business for an amount of time, and then you might wish to have the business pay it back to you at another time. You must keep track of this so that the funds don't get confused as income to the business or income to you later.

For this, I use what I call a **to/from account**, classified as an equity account if you are using accounting software. You will see this account on your **Balance Sheet**, but not on your Profit/Loss Statement. This account tracks when you invest money into your company, and when the company pays you back. Some people like to create a loan, and then have the company pay interest back. If you are a sole proprietor, I find this a little redundant as you will get the deduction as an expense in your business, but you will have to claim it on your personal taxes as income. If you have partners then it might be a good idea, so that the financial side is accurate and fair for all parties involved.

Always remember to **keep your business and personal expenses separate**. The IRS says that you may expense the money that runs your business, but paying for your kid to go to a soccer game is not something that runs your business, so you can't class it as a business expense. You must keep this completely separate from your business money. You can give your company some money, and your company can give the money back to you, but you don't want to run your personal expenses through the business. However, if you want to sponsor your child's team, for advertising purposes, this is a legal and legitimate way to run an expense through your business.

Going back to Bob's BBQ Joint, in the deep dive we also discovered that Bob would purchase household supplies & groceries for his home directly from his supplier using the business money. This is a problem on multiple levels. Most importantly, he has co-mingled personal with business. Now, he cannot accurately determine the restaurant's food cost, or overhead expenses. And, if the IRS were to audit the books and catch this, he could be on the hook for having a bigger profit and having a larger tax bill + penalties. This makes budgeting and cash flow planning very difficult when you want solid numbers for your business. Breaking down costs enough to know if you are actually charging enough for that rack of ribs, or that pulled pork sandwich. Feed your family from your profit!

In some businesses, this can cause a business to be so out of touch with its numbers that it could end up closing its doors, or worse, never really being able to "pay yourself" a paycheck. Remember why you went into business? The goal was to do something you love, and replace and increase your income from your day job.

SIMPLIFYING YOUR DATA

I highly recommend that you **get a good accounting/bookkeeping software**. Yes, you can do the whole thing on a checking account and register (Hello, 1960's!), or if you're an Excel wizard, by keeping scrupulously exact spreadsheets (Hello 1980s!). But, I subscribe to the KISS method: "Keep It Simple, Stupid." No, I'm not calling you stupid, but we tend to overcomplicate things and feel stupid.

Bookkeeping software is made specifically for that job, and not only does it make it easy for you to get those four statements out of your basic information, but later it will help you to grow as a business. You won't have to figure out how to get everything into the software after the business gets too big to work on spreadsheets (or pay your CPA $150-200 an hour to do it for you). It's an expense that I think is easily justified from the beginning, especially now that there are online packages that you can pay for month to month.

QuickBooks is the industry gold standard, although there are other packages out there that people like. I don't personally recommend QuickBooks Online, as I find it cumbersome and unwieldy. (But I'll admit that I'm not the sort of person who lives online and loves the latest technology.) And I really don't recommend Quicken for Business, as you will outgrow it well before you will want to.

A quick note: if you are using any other kinds of programs (such as project management or customer management software packages) that need to interface with your bookkeeping, you'll want to make sure that they can be integrated together. This will cut down on double entering data and limit mistakes.

You will pay for accounting and bookkeeping now, or you will pay for it later. Paying for a software package that works for you now means you won't have to pay to recreate everything in the future. You *can* mess up in QuickBooks, but it's also much easier for your bookkeeper and/or accountant to un-scramble those problems in QuickBooks.

FINANCIALS

When you start a business, and enter your information into your software, you've done a number of things almost automatically. You will put money into the checking account, and then enter your expenses going out from that account: your software purchase, your checks, maybe buying a mobile phone for the business.

You can then click a couple of menu items and generate that **Balance Sheet** (with the asset of the capital input that you have given your business) and a **Profit/Loss Statement**. (These are simple reports/statements that any software program can run for you.) You can easily balance your bank accounts. You can also budget directly from QuickBooks.

Look at you go!

Keep in mind, you may not necessarily *need* all four kinds of statements. If you really can manage your money by your checkbook, your Profit/Loss Statement, and your Balance Sheet, then don't muddy the waters any more than necessary. (KISS again!)

I do recommend that you learn to use these statements and be able to read them now, while they're still simple. You will have fewer problems working with them later when your business is bigger and those statements are more complicated.

Now that you have your Balance Sheet and Profit/Loss Statement, you can easily figure out your **Budget**.

Your Budget is you telling your money what you want your money to do, and how much you want to spend on categories. Your budget says, "I want to spend X number of dollars for office expenses, X number of dollars for supplies, X number of dollars for transportation, and X number of dollars for advertising/marketing."

For instance, I have a category in my budget for conferences. If I've planned the conference budget for $3,000 this year, and the first conference of the year is $1,500, I know I'm already halfway into my budget. I can decide if I want to go to that one conference or get more bang for my conference money if I went to three different, smaller conferences for $500 each. Incidentally, it's also a great tool for when sales people call you and want to sell you something. You can say, "Sorry, it's not in the budget!" It's amazing how people who otherwise won't take "no" for an answer will understand "it's not in the budget!"

Remember, the budget looks and feels like it's set in stone, but, like just about everything else, it's not really set in stone. You can change a budget at any time, because once you know your numbers you'll know how you need to change them. Are you meeting your goals, are you exceeding your goals, are you not there yet? You can move money allocated for one item to another when you need to do so.

Budgets are a great tool for helping you to decide where you want your money to go, but you rule your budget, it does not rule you. When you know your numbers, you can make educated decisions for your budget as you go along.

We now have our Balance Sheet, our Profit/Loss Statement, and our Budget. The **Cash Flow Statement** takes the information from all three of the other statements and brings them together to show you how the money is flowing through your business.

Let's say that you've just started by personally adding $1,000 into the business. You need to buy a copy of QuickBooks, some office supplies, and your cell phone. You now have $400 leftover—where in your business do you want that $400 to flow? What else do you need to buy, or otherwise spend the money on, or do you need to save that $400 for the next month because you know you'll have your cell phone bill and other expenses coming?

Your cash flow is, "Here is my money that is available to use, and this is where my Budget says I should use it, and this is how it flows from place to place."

Typically, a cash flow is month-to-month or week-to-week depending on the volume and detail of your business needs.

Remember that cash flow may not be an expense, and it may not be income, but it is flowing through your business. Perhaps that $400 leftover can now be paid back because your business will generate income, which will bring the bank account total higher again, leaving a surplus. Maybe you will want to keep that money in the emergency fund or Sinking Fund until your company is completely stable and can pay you back at a later date.

OTHER REPORTS

Every business is going to need to run other reports besides our big four to keep their business on the right track.

Most retail and service businesses will need to run a daily report that breaks down income and expenses. This is especially useful when collecting sales tax or using petty cash (or a cash drawer). Sales tax is money you collect on behalf of the city, county, and state. It isn't really your money so you don't want to classify that as income. You will also want to break out service sales from product sales, again, because service sales are generally not subject to sales tax.

Your daily report might look like this:

Daily Report		
	Amount	**Notes**
DAILY INCOME		
Product Sales	_____	_____
Service Sales	_____	_____
Sales Tax Collected	_____	_____
Total Income	_____	_____
DAILY EXPENDITURES		
Food Truck - COD		
Advertising	_____	*Soccer Tourament Sponsorship*
Petty Cash	_____	_____
Total Cash Out	_____	_____
DAILY DEPOSITS		
Cash/Check	_____	*Taken to Bank*
Credit/Debit Card	_____	*Electronic Deposit*

(This is a great way to separate into your Sinking Fund and to save for next month/quarter when this tax is due).

You can list other transactions if it's helpful to you or your bookkeeper—such as hand-written checks to the post office.

Then, total up your day's expenses: the COD for the food delivery was cash that went to the delivery driver, and you'll need to show that cash outgo. Once you have added up and subtracted out everything, the number below the line should be what you need to deposit to the bank at the end of the business day.

This will help you with two things: First, are you bringing in more money than you are sending out? Second, are you on track for your daily sales, or do you need to beef up sales tomorrow, or maybe lower expenses?

A daily sheet is another fantastic tool for you to keep your business on track. Keep in mind that KISS applies here too—you are going to be busy with marketing, growing your business, managing your business, your team, and dealing with surprise issues that come up, so you want to be able to see the bottom line of your daily sheets at a glance.

BOB'S BBQ, LLC
Profit/Loss Worksheet (Pre-Coaching)

INCOME

Deposits

Cash/Checks Deposited	$	104,095.80 A
Credit/Debit Deposits	$	142,506.00
Total Deposits	**$**	**246,601.80**

Cost of Goods Sold

Cost of Goods Sold	$	75,145.81
Total Cost of Goods Sold	**$**	**75,145.81**

TOTAL INCOME	$	171,455.99

EXPENSES

Expenses

Automobile	$	1,664.80
Bank Charges	$	303.00
Depreciation	$	575.00
Insurance	$	2,835.00
Repairs	$	1,278.90
Interest Expense	$	3,854.13
Supplies	$	295.87
Legal Fees	$	375.00
Rent	$	2,400.00
Payroll Expenses	$	85,243.15
Gas and Electric	$	1,614.95
Telephone	$	684.86
Water	$	446.23
Total Expenses	**$**	**101,570.89**

TOTAL EXPENSES	$	101,570.89

BALANCE	**$**	**69,885.10**

* *The Four Walls*

Notes

A: Includes $40k Bob put into the business and a $40k loan

IT'S YOUR TURN

Look at the Pre-Coaching example of Bob's BBQ Joint. What Red Flags are you seeing in Bob's Profit/Loss Statement?

_____

_____

_____

_____

_____

It looks like Bob made a profit. Did he really? Why or why not?

_____

_____

_____

_____

_____

_____

Share your answers online at RockinYourBusinessFinances.com to enter to win a free hour of Small Biz Coaching.

The Post-Coaching report that follows shows a better, more detailed layout.

BOB'S BBQ, LLC
Profit/Loss Worksheet (Post-Coaching)

INCOME		
Food Truck Income		
Catering	$	33,463.39
Special Events	$	12,543.50
Festivals	$	3,500.00
Other Income	$	-
Other Income	$	-
Total Food Truck Income	$	**49,506.89**
Restaurant Income		
Beverages	$	7,514.95
Kids/Senior Meals	$	9,918.39
Military Meals	$	5,141.30
Regular Meals	$	68,591.50
To Go Orders	$	25,928.77
Total Restaurant Income	$	**117,094.91**
TOTAL INCOME	$ - $ -	$ 166,601.80
COST OF GOODS SOLD (COGS)		
Cost of Goods Sold		
Delivery Fee	$	175.00
* Food Costs	$	74,970.81
Other COGS	$	-
Total Cost of Goods Sold	$	**75,145.81**
TOTAL COGS	$ - $ -	$ 75,145.81
GROSS PROFIT	$ - $ -	$ 91,455.99
EXPENSES		
Payroll Expenses		
Bookkeeper	$	10,000.00
* Kitchen Staff	$	45,200.00
* Wait Staff	$	20,043.15
Owner/Manager	$	10,000.00 B
Total Payroll	$	**85,243.15**

Automobile		
Fuel	$	982.68
Insurance	$	427.62
Maintenance & Repairs	$	254.50
Other	$	-
Total Automobile	**$**	**1,664.80**
Depreciation		
Truck	$	575.00
Kitchen Equipment	$	-
Other	$	-
Total Depreciation	**$**	**575.00**
Insurance		
Liability	$	1,005.00
* Worker's Comp	$	1,830.00
Other	$	-
Total Insurance	**$**	**2,835.00**
Operating Expenses		
Bank Service Charges	$	303.00
Equipment Repairs	$	1,278.90
Interest Expense	$	3,854.13 A
Office Supplies	$	295.87
Professional Legal/Acctg	$	375.00
Rent	$	2,400.00
Total Operating Expenses	**$**	**8,506.90**
Utilities		
* Gas and Electric	$	1,614.95
Telephone	$	684.86
* Water	$	446.23
Extra for Debt Payments	$	1,500.00
Total Utilities	**$**	**4,246.04**
TOTAL EXPENSES	**$ - $ -**	**$ 103,070.89**
NET INCOME	**$ - $ -**	**$ (11,614.90)**

* *The Four Walls*

Notes

A: True Interest Expense

B: See Pay Yourself

Profit/Loss Worksheet

INCOME

Income A

1) _____ $ -
2) _____ $ -
3) _____ $ -
4) _____ $ -
5) _____ $ -

Total Income A $ -

Income B

1) _____ $ -
2) _____ $ -
3) _____ $ -
4) _____ $ -
5) _____ $ -

Total Income B $ -

TOTAL INCOME $ - $ - $ -

COST OF GOODS SOLD (COGS)

Cost of Goods Sold

1) _____ $ -
2) _____ $ -
3) _____ $ -

Total Cost of Goods Sold $ -

TOTAL COGS $ - $ - $ -

GROSS PROFIT $ - $ - $ -

EXPENSES

Payroll Expenses

1) _____ $ -
2) _____ $ -
3) _____ $ -
4) _____ $ -

Total Payroll $ -

Expense A

1) _____	$	-
2) _____	$	-
3) _____	$	-
4) _____	$	-
Total Expense A	**$**	**-**

Expense B

1) _____	$	-
2) _____	$	-
3) _____	$	-
Total Expense B	**$**	**-**

Expense C

1) _____	$	-
2) _____	$	-
3) _____	$	-
Total Expense C	**$**	**-**

Operating Expenses

1) _____	$	-
2) _____	$	-
3) _____	$	-
4) _____	$	-
5) _____	$	-
6) _____	$	-
Total Operating Expenses	**$**	**-**

Utilities

1) _____	$	-
2) _____	$	-
3) _____	$	-
4) _____	$	-
Total Utilities	**$**	**-**

TOTAL EXPENSES	**$**	**-**	**$**	**-**	**$**	**-**

NET INCOME	**$**	**-**	**$**	**-**	**$**	**-**

* *The Four Walls*

Notes

A:

B:

BOB'S BBQ, LLC
Monthly Budget

	Regular	Irregular (Annual)
INCOME		
Food Truck Income		
Catering	$ 60,000.00	
Special Events	$ 10,000.00	
Festivals	$ 5,000.00	
Other Income	$ -	
Other Income	$ -	
Total Food Truck Income	$ 75,000.00	$ -
Restaurant Income		
Beverages	$ 10,000.00	
Kids/Senior Meals	$ 15,000.00	
Military Meals	$ 2,000.00	
Regular Meals	$ 85,000.00	
To Go Orders	$ 20,000.00	
Total Restaurant Income	$ 132,000.00	$ -
TOTAL INCOME	$ 207,000.00	$ -
COST OF GOODS SOLD (COGS)		
Cost of Goods Sold		
Delivery Fee	$ 200.00	
* Food Costs	$ 62,100.00	
Other COGS	$ -	
Total Cost of Goods Sold	$ 62,300.00	$ -
TOTAL COGS	$ 62,300.00	$ -
GROSS PROFIT	$ 144,700.00	$ -
EXPENSES		
Payroll Expenses		
Bookkeeper	$ 6,000.00	
* Kitchen Staff	$ 85,000.00	
* Wait Staff	$ 20,000.00	
Owner/Manager	$ 10,000.00	
Total Payroll	$ 121,000.00	$ -

Automobile				
Fuel	$	800.00		
Insurance	$	200.00	$	2,400.00
Maintenance & Repairs	$	100.00	$	1,200.00
Other	$	-		
Total Automobile	**$**	**1,100.00**	**$**	**3,600.00**
Depreciation				
Truck	$	300.00		
Kitchen Equipment	$	275.00		
Other	$	-		
Total Depreciation	**$**	**575.00**	**$**	**-**
Insurance				
Liability	$	83.75	$	1,005.00
* Worker's Comp	$	152.50	$	1,830.00
Other	$	-		
Total Insurance	**$**	**236.25**	**$**	**2,835.00**
Operating Expenses				
Bank Service Charges	$	120.00		
Equipment Repairs	$	1,000.00		
Interest Expense	$	2,500.00		
Office Supplies	$	300.00		
Professional Legal/Acctg	$	375.00		
Rent	$	2,400.00		
Total Operating Expenses	**$**	**6,695.00**	**$**	**-**
Utilities				
* Gas and Electric	$	1,700.00		
Telephone	$	700.00		
* Water	$	500.00		
Debt Payments ($975 extra)	$	1,500.00		
Total Utilities	**$**	**4,400.00**	**$**	**-**
TOTAL EXPENSES	**$**	**134,006.25**		
NET INCOME	**$**	**10,693.75**		

* *The Four Walls*

Monthly Budget

	Regular		Irregular (Annual)	
INCOME				
Income A:				
1)	$	-		
2)	$	-		
3)	$	-		
4)	$	-		
5)	$	-		
Total Income A	$	-	$	-
Income B:				
1)	$	-		
2)	$	-		
3)	$	-		
4)	$	-		
5)	$	-		
Total Income B	$	-	$	-
TOTAL INCOME	$	-	$	-
COST OF GOODS SOLD (COGS)				
Cost of Goods Sold				
1)	$	-		
2)	$	-		
3)	$	-		
Total Cost of Goods Sold	$	-	$	-
TOTAL COGS	$	-	$	-
GROSS PROFIT	$	-	$	-
EXPENSES				
Payroll Expenses				
1)	$	-		
2)	$	-		
3)	$	-		
4)	$	-		
Total Payroll	$	-	$	-

Expense A		
1)	$ -	
2)	$ -	
3)	$ -	
4)	$ -	
Total Expense A	**$ -**	**$ -**
Expense B		
1)	$ -	
2)	$ -	
3)	$ -	
Total Expense B	**$ -**	**$ -**
Expense C		
1)	$ -	
2)	$ -	
3)	$ -	
Total Expense C	**$ -**	**$ -**
Operating Expenses		
1)	$ -	
2)	$ -	
3)	$ -	
4)	$ -	
5)	$ -	
6)	$ -	
Total Operating Expenses	**$ -**	**$ -**
Utilities		
1)	$ -	
2)	$ -	
3)	$ -	
4)	$ -	
Total Utilities	**$ -**	**$ -**
TOTAL EXPENSES	**$ -**	
NET INCOME	**$ -**	

*** The Four Walls**

BOB'S BBQ, LLC
Balance Sheet

		Year
ASSETS		
Current Assets		
Cash Accounts		
Checking	$	3,428.96
Savings – Emergency	$	5,987.50
Savings – Sinking Fund	$	10,325.23
Total Cash Accounts	$	**19,741.69**
Accounts Receivable		
Accounts Receivable	$	18,540.63
Total Accounts Receiveable	$	**18,540.63**
Other Current Assets		
Inventory Assets	$	4,506.10
Undeposited Funds	$	110.00
Total Other Current Assets	$	**4,616.10**
Total Current Assets	$	**42,898.42**
Fixed Assets		
Assets		
Equipment	$	5,190.11
Food Truck	$	32,826.07
Accumulated Depreciation	$	(1,725.00)
Original Purchase	$	34,551.07
Total Fixed Assets	$	**38,016.18**
TOTAL ASSETS	$	**80,914.60**

LIABILITIES & EQUITY		
Liabilities		
Current Liabilities		
Accounts Payable	$	2,578.69
Credit Card	$	1,473.99
Short Term Liabilities	$	6,162.26
Payroll Liabilities	$	4,558.68
Sales Tax Payable	$	1,603.58
Total Current Liabilities	**$**	**10,214.94**
Long Term Liabilities		
DEBT – Bank Loans	$	77,593.97
Equipment Loan	$	3,911.32
Operating Loan	$	40,000.00
Truck Loan	$	33,682.65
Total Long Term Liabilities	**$**	**77,593.97**
Total Liabilities	**$**	**87,808.91**
Equity		
Owner's Equity		
Owner's Contributions	$	40,000.00
Owner's Draw	$	(79,234.07)
Total Owner's Equity	**$**	**(39,234.07)**
Retained Earnings	$	43,954.66
Net Income	$	(11,614.90)
Total Equity	**$**	**(6,894.31)**
TOTAL LIABILITIES AND EQUITY	$	80,914.60
BALANCE (should be zero)	$	-

Balance Sheet

	Year	
ASSETS		
Current Assets		
Cash Accounts		
Checking	$	-
Savings – Emergency	$	-
Savings – Sinking Fund	$	-
Total Cash Accounts	$	-
Accounts Receivable		
Accounts Receivable	$	-
Total Accounts Receiveable	$	-
Other Current Assets		
Inventory Assets	$	-
Undeposited Funds	$	-
Total Other Current Assets	$	-
Total Current Assets	$	-
Fixed Assets		
Assets		
1)	$	-
2)	$	-
3)	$	-
4)	$	-
Total Fixed Assets	$	-
TOTAL ASSETS	$	-

LIABILITIES & EQUITY		
Liabilities		
Current Liabilities		
Accounts Payable	$	-
Credit Card	$	-
Short Term Liabilities	$	-
Payroll Liabilities	$	-
Sales Tax Payable	$	-
Total Current Liabilities	**$**	**-**
Long Term Liabilities		
DEBT – Bank Loans	$	-
1)	$	-
2)	$	-
3)	$	-
Total Long Term Liabilities	**$**	**-**
Total Liabilities	**$**	**-**
Equity		
Owner's Equity		
Owner's Contributions	$	-
Owner's Draw	$	-
Total Owner's Equity	**$**	**-**
Retained Earnings	$	-
Net Income	$	-
Total Equity	**$**	**-**
TOTAL LIABILITIES AND EQUITY	**$**	**-**
BALANCE (should be zero)	**$**	**-**

IT'S YOUR TURN

What financial reports have you used to date and how do you use them?

_____

_____

_____

_____

_____

Which of the financial reports in this chapter feel most helpful?

_____

_____

_____

_____

_____

_____

Do you have the systems in place to generate the reports on a consistent basis?

_____

_____

_____

_____

_____

How comfortable do you feel using them? What questions do you have?

_____

_____

_____

_____

_____

_____

_____

Where can you find the resources you need to professionally run your business?

_____

_____

_____

_____

_____

_____

_____

For FREE Spreadsheets and Forms,
visit RockinYourBusinessFinances.com.

CHAPTER 5
PAYING YOURSELF

In Chapter 3, we talked a little about how your business might be able to legally pay for things that you had to pay for yourself as a wage earner. Before your business, you might have been paying for your cell phone. The business may be able to cover that now (depending upon your personal use of the phone), or cover the cost of a new phone, because now you might need a smart phone where before a 'dumb' phone was plenty. Perhaps you have a home office now, and you may be able to reimburse yourself for some of your internet and utilities or, in some cases, pay yourself rent to help cover some of those costs. You may be able to pay yourself for mileage for business-related travel, or possibly your business may be able to own your vehicle and pay for its upkeep, fuel, insurance, and depreciation.

There's a little-known IRS rule which says, "If you need a uniform, your business can pay for it." You get a polo shirt, put your name on the polo shirt, and you wear it everywhere while on the job. That's your uniform. If you like polo shirts, you're personally not paying for those anymore and the IRS says that that's okay, because you are advertising your business.

THE TAX MENTALITY

Your home budget is a lot higher as a wage earner because you didn't have any business expenses. Your personal budget might be a lot less expensive as a self-employed person because your business is now covering some of those expenses. You are no longer trying to replace that wage earner income, you're trying to figure out how much you need to earn in your business by knowing how much you need to take home to cover your personal bills. That is a *tax mentality*.

You need to know how much is needed to cover the personal expenses that your business won't be covering. The type of business organization will then become key to your tax burdens and how your cash flow works for you.

LLCS, LLPS, S CORPS, AND DBAS

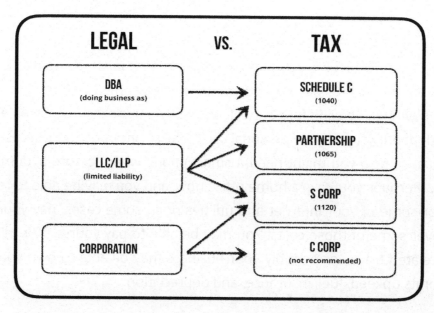

Understanding the Legal vs. the Tax of your business. When I start working with a business client I always ask, "What is the legal set up of your company?"

"I'm an LLC!"

"Great, now how do you file your taxes?"

"Ummm..."

An LLC or LLP means Limited Liability Company or Limited Liability Partnership. That "limited liability" is the important concept. You've separated your personal self from your business. The company is over there and you're over here. You've limited your personal risk, but you need to make decisions about how you're going to treat your taxes.

Limited liability companies can file taxes in three different ways. A Schedule C on your 1040 return as a DBA, Form 1065 as a Partnership or Form 1120S as an S Corp.

You can file a Schedule C, which is the same as being a DBA, I did this for years and don't recommend it because you're paying self-employment tax on all profit. Unless of course your business is very small and you really don't plan for it to be much more than a hobby.

A partnership or an LLP means that it's not just you. It means that you've got another human being or entity that shares in the business. Parenthetically, be careful because in my experience a lot of partnerships sink unless you're married to the partner. An ironclad partnership agreement might allow for a partnership that works, if you're willing to bring in a lawyer. A partnership is also going to pay all that tax, again, because the profit is split between the partners, and flows through to the 1040 tax. All the partners must pay the self-employment tax if they are materially participating in the business. This can get a little messy and confusing if you have a 'silent' partner. You will file what's called a 1065 Partnership Return. Each partner will receive a K-1 form based on that return. Lines from the K-1 will be reflected on the front page of your 1040 as business profit or loss. And then, self-employment tax will be added to your liability accordingly.

If you're a Schedule C (DBA) or a partnership, your clients, by law, give you a 1099 form at the end of the year, which means they must report to the IRS how much money they paid you. If you're an S Corp, they are not required to do that, as the IRS believes that an S Corp is more likely to claim all income.

You could be a Limited Liability Company and file your taxes as an S Corp. You'll have a Form 1120 tax return. All the shareholders/members of your company will get a Form K-1 which reports profit separately from W2 wages as part of your whole tax documents. Your company will also give you a W2 as a wage earner. If you use the strategies noted earlier in this chapter then you will hit, "the making more as a business owner by making less as a wage earner" that typically saves you the most in taxes.

THE MIGHTY S CORP

When we are in business, we should pay ourselves. But, repeatedly, I see the same crazy thing happening: we go into business for ourselves, we put all our money back into our business, and we don't get anything to take home. Who can live like that?

It comes down to not understanding how to pay yourself, and that's where the S Corp, which I recommend whenever possible, comes in. Now you have at least a basic understanding with the definitions of DBA, LLC, and S Corp companies. If you'd like to dig deeper, Google it and come right back.

If you are a DBA, you are "Doing Business As" you, an individual, then you track all your income minus all your expenses. Not loan repayments (only the interest portion), not business repayments, but "income minus expenses equals profit." The profit is taxed as self-employment income, which means you'll pay federal tax, state tax (if your state has income tax—seven states currently don't have an income tax: Alaska, Florida, Nevada, South Dakota, Texas, Washington, and Wyoming. Residents of New Hampshire and Tennessee pay tax on dividends and income from investments, but no income tax), FICA = Social Security tax, and Medicare tax.

If you are operating as a DBA, you pay your personal share of Medicare tax and Social Security tax and for Medicare and Social Security as the employer. Where you were paying 7.65%, multiply by two, and now you're paying 15.3%. That's the self-employment tax: Medicare plus Social Security.

In numbers, what that 15.3% means is that if you made a profit of $100,000, then you're paying $15,300 for FICA (employee and employer).

Some of my clients will say, "I don't know if I should even bother being an S Corp. If I must pay both sides of the Social Security/Medicare then it's the same thing, right?" In this example, it is clearly not the same thing.

If the business is an S Corp, then it pays taxes a little bit differently. As per IRS guidelines an S Corp owner must get paid a reasonable wage. This means "If you were going to hire somebody to do the job that you're doing for the company, what would you pay that person to do that job?"

The IRS loosely defines that as 50% of profit—remember that's after all those business expenses are paid. If you are the president of the company that just made a profit of $100,000, then it's reasonable, at a bare minimum, that you would pay the *president* of that company $50,000. As the *owner* of the company, the other ½ of that profit $50,000 is return on investment.

Looking through the lens of a tax mentality, if you pay yourself a reasonable wage of $50,000 and pay self-employment tax on that $50,000, then you would pay $7,650 ($50,000 x 15.3%). You save the other $7,650 from the profit because that is not included in your wages. You are only paying self-employment tax on the reasonable wage.

You want to make a profit, but you don't want to pay any more in tax than you absolutely must. To summarize—same business same profit, but not the same tax. The non-S Corp pays $15,300 in FICA, the S Corp owner (reasonable wage) only pays $7,650 in FICA. The savings doesn't stop there—you will still have to pay Federal & State taxes. Look at the Making More by Making Less chart below you will see how there are potentially additional savings in Federal & State taxes.

MAKING MORE BY MAKING LESS

As we take the deep dive into the Mighty S Corp, the chart below is the illustration of the tax savings. Take a minute to try this formula out on your own numbers so you can see the potential tax savings for yourself.

The bottom line is this: you need a great tax professional and a tax mentality. There are great savings to be had when you pay attention to the tax ramifications of your business strategies. Choose your tax structure based on what works best for your company. Pay yourself based on the profits—not just a random number in your head. Ultimately, by allowing your business to pay its honest share of expenses, build in retirement and benefit plans, and pay taxes through payroll, you will need less in a paycheck while enjoying more as a successful business owner.

THE MATH
Making More by Making Less

DBA/PARTNERSHIP vs. THE MIGHTY S CORP

	DBA/PARTNERSHIP		S CORP	
Profit from Business Activities		$ 100,000.00		$ 100,000.00
Taxable Income from Business	100.00%	$ 100,000.00	50.00%	$ 50,000.00
Owner Salary (reasonable wage)	0.00%	$ -	50.00%	$ 50,000.00
Taxes on Owner Salary	**Tax Rate**	**Total Tax**	**Tax Rate**	**Total Tax**
Employer Payroll (FICA) on Salary	0.00%	$ -	7.65%	$ (3,825.00)
Total Taxes on Owner Salary		$ -		$ (3,825.00)
Tax Calculation	**Tax Rate**	**Total Tax**	**Tax Rate**	**Total Tax**
Profit after Owner Salary		$ 100,000.00		$ 46,175.00
Self Employment Tax Rate	15.30%	$ (15,300.00)	0.00%	$ -
Federal Tax Rate (varies)	20.00%	$ (20,000.00)	20.00%	$ (9,235.00)
State Tax Rate (varies)	5.00%	$ (5,000.00)	5.00%	$ (2,308.75)
Total Taxes Paid (on Profit)		$ (40,300.00)		$ (11,543.75)
Salary Taxes	**Tax Rate**	**Total Tax**	**Tax Rate**	**Total Tax**
Owner Salary		$ -		$ 50,000.00
Self Employment Tax Rate	15.30%	$ -	7.65%	$ (3,825.00)
Federal Tax Rate (varies)	20.00%	$ -	20.00%	$ (10,000.00)
State Tax Rate (varies)	5.00%	$ -	5.00%	$ (2,500.00)
Total Salary Taxes Paid		$ -		$ (16,325.00)
TOTAL PROFIT		$ 100,000.00		$ 100,000.00
TOTAL TAXES		$ (40,300.00)		$ (31,693.75)
TOTAL TAKE HOME INCOME		$ 59,700.00		$ 68,306.25
		THE MIGHTY S CORP SAVINGS =		**$ 8,606.25**

S CORP AND RETIREMENT

The most fun of the S Corp equation is retirement. (This can be done for the other business entities, it's just a little bit more convoluted.) If you slide a retirement plan in there for yourself, which is part of the "paying yourself more by paying yourself less" equation, you can save even more on federal and state tax. You won't save yourself self-employment tax, but you can save on your federal and state because retirement plans, in most cases, are going to be a pre-tax deduction.

I, generally, recommend that you do the pre-tax investing within your business and then the Roth IRA tax from the personal side. (If you are making more than the Roth IRA limit on the personal side, then this is a different discussion). As with all taxable events, you should chat with your CPA to get the best fit for your situation.

Let's go back to our $100,000 profit. You're paying yourself $50,000 as your wage, but you're going to do a SIMPLE IRA, which you can max out. As of 2017, if you're under fifty, you can contribute $12,500 per year. If you're over fifty, you may make a catch-up contribution up to $3000 (subject to cost of living adjustments for later years).

What does that mean? Let's say you're 50 and you are investing in yourself in the form of a retirement plan. Based on our $100,000 profit figure, divide that in half, and you're paying yourself a wage of $50,000. Then, take out $15,500. Now, your wage drops down to $34,500. You haven't replaced your income. You're making $34,500 on the payroll side and you're taxed less, but don't forget that you've got that $50,000 profit on the other side that's not payroll-related.

That's all profit. That can come out of the business any time you want in the form of draws. Yes, you'll be subject to federal and state tax on that money (and might need to make estimated tax payments), but you've just saved whatever your tax rate is on the $15,500 retirement contribution.

If you're at a 30% tax bracket, you've just saved an additional $4,650 ($15,500 x 30% by investing in yourself and lowering your tax liability.

The cool part with the SIMPLE IRA is that your company can now match 3% of the $50,000 which is another $1,500 that goes into your SIMPLE IRA, and another $450 in tax savings.

I am a fan of the SIMPLE IRA for many reasons. I like the tax laws that require you to offer the same plan to your employees. It's an awesome benefit. Each of your employees can get the same tax benefits with tax deductions and you are only required to match up to an additional 3%; it's not a lot of money out of your pocket, but for your employee it's an amazing benefit. (See more on retirement in Chapter 8.)

S CORP AND SOCIAL SECURITY PAYOUTS

Here's the concern I get from clients, and I get it a lot, "Well, if I'm not paying that much into Social Security I won't get that much out of Social Security." Ah, that's a good point. An excellent point, but I've done the math on that and there's only so much you can get out of Social Security anyway.

Also, if you put more money into your own retirement, do you need to worry about Social Security? This is where you get to plan your own retirement. This is where you get to say, "Social Security is going to be play money, WOO HOO!"

Social Security has always been a political football, depending on who you talk to it will either be here at retirement or it won't. There are formulas when to take it and when not, and then there are the assumptions on how long you live as to how much you will gain benefits from. If you are investing in your own retirement savings plans, then this alleviates some of those concerns on how much is enough.

S CORP AND QUARTERLY TAXES

The nice thing about paying yourself a reasonable wage is that as long as you hit the last day of the year, and you've paid that reasonable wage, it's all cool. You don't have to pay yourself all that much money in the very beginning if you're not going to have all that much money in the very end. In contrast, all DBA businesses are required to pay quarterly estimated taxes—this is the estimated tax you think you will owe based on each quarter of the year. Remember, your taxes are Self-Employment (FICA 15.3%) plus federal tax at your rate; then state tax if applicable. The IRS requires quarterly estimated payments, those amounts are based on your prior years' sales. Each quarter you must send a payment of ¼ of your annual tax to the government. If the bulk of your sales are in the end of the year, you still must send those quarterly payments at the beginning and middle of the year.

As an S Corp, that's not necessary. You just should pay yourself at a bare minimum at least once a quarter, and file your payroll reports at least once a quarter. If your slowest months are January through March, you just should pay yourself a little bit so you have a quarterly report. If April through June is booming you'd pay more. And, you can pay yourself big paychecks at the end of the year in the form of bonuses. This is where knowing your numbers works in your favor. Remember you are paying yourself a reasonable wage based on profit. If you don't have a profit in a quarter you can file a zero payroll, just be sure that you don't do this every quarter, remember you are in business to make a profit!

The other fun thing you can do (and this is only possible if your home budget is turn-key, it must be perfect to do this) is to only pay yourself once a quarter. That lowers your paperwork significantly. You may pay all your employees as often as you want. If you have employees and you're an S Corp, you can pay them weekly, bi-weekly, twice a month, monthly, whatever you want to do. You are not required by law to stay on one payroll schedule over another. Nor, as the owner, are you required to be on the same payroll schedule as your employees.

In the S Corp environment, where your overall profit can be significant, which could put you back in the quarterly estimates if you owe more in taxes, you can pay that additional tax in your payroll checks. That way you don't have to remember the quarterly reporting dates, as it comes out of your regular payroll checks. For me, this simplifies the tax process. I get a reasonable wage, get to fully fund my retirement, pay my taxes on time, and, although my actual paychecks might be less than as an employee, as a business owner, I am realizing return on investment.

BARTERING

A regular customer of Bob's BBQ Joint is a massage therapist. She has come to you with a "great idea". She wants you to trade out some catering for a party she's throwing in exchange for some much-needed massage therapy. This is one of those classic places where we tend to barter our services. It feels like a natural way to get paid without getting paid. The IRS truly frowns upon bartering, because what they want is to see the income and expenses on the massage therapist's side and the income and expenses on the restaurant's side.

You need to be very careful. If you get audited, you will want to be able to show the IRS trackable proof of the trading you've done on services because if you don't, the IRS may tell you that you need to pay taxes on the income from those services. They may decide the massage services are personal, not business related, and there may be taxes on any income spent or expensed. If your massage therapist is expensive, $150 for an hour massage, or you inflate it to make it even, then that's a high risk for you.

I don't recommend you do much bartering. Instead you might trade an hour's massage for an hour of cooking, or keep it simply friends helping friends. There's nothing wrong with a massage therapist giving a friend a massage, and there's nothing wrong with a friend giving some barbequed brisket to a friend. Keep it at, "I have a customer, she's a massage therapist," so you'll need to charge each other for those services, or keep it on a friend's basis only.

Also, keep in mind that most bartering never turns out exactly even on both sides. Often it ruins not only the business relationship, but also friendships.

IT'S YOUR TURN

Do you have a tax mentality? Why or why not?

_____

_____

_____

_____

_____

_____

Where do you see that you can bring home less, but have the same lifestyle?
(Think of items that are truly Business Expenses.)

_____

_____

_____

_____

_____

_____

_____

_____

What LEGAL structure do you have in place now? How are you filing your taxes?

_____

_____

_____

_____

_____

What potential improvements do you see?

_____

_____

_____

_____

_____

_____

_____

_____

This might be a GREAT time to schedule a meeting with your CPA to discuss this chapter.

For FREE Spreadsheets and Forms, including the Making More by Making Less Worksheet, visit RockinYourBusinessFinances.com.

CHAPTER 6
OPERATING DEBT FREE

The best way to run a business is debt free. Debt means that you are chasing money backwards. You're already in a hole, and you need to fill that hole before you can step on that ground to move on.

The concept of using debt as a tool, interest on debt as a business expense, debt as a deduction off your taxes, and debt as capital input, are all myths designed by banks to sell their product called loans. They make their profit on the debt interest that you pay back. Debt is not necessary to start and grow most businesses.

At times, you may feel that you must have debt to grow, but it's got to be in your budget not only to make the payments, but to make *extra* payments. You've got to get that debt out of your way, so that your money can do what it's designed to do, make a profit for you. Until then, you're paying the bank to be in business.

If you decide that there's no way to open your business without debt, then make sure that it leaves your life as quickly as possible. If you don't, your business leaving your life will become much more likely, and no one wants that.

A CAUTIONARY TALE

I knew a woman who wanted to open a veterinary clinic. Like many new businesses, she didn't have clients yet. So, she didn't have any money coming in to purchase equipment or to operate her business and not enough savings to purchase those things outright. She did have one of the best written business plans I'd ever seen. Her bank agreed, and loaned her money on the strength of it. She got that loan under the Small Business Administration (SBA) loan program, and pledged her house and retirement as additional collateral when she signed for the loan.

She used part of the loan to lease a building for the clinic, plus equipment, only to find out after purchasing all the equipment it only interfaced with PC computers—but all her computers were Apple. To cope with that, she hired an IT contractor to make her equipment talk to her computers, using up another $40,000 of her loan. (Needless to say, none of these things were in her business plan other than the purchase of the equipment.)

Now she had used the bulk of her loan, including the portion that was intended to cover operating costs for the first year. She didn't even come close to following her business plan. After less than a year, the clinic had to close, and the bank took its collateral back on the loan in the form of her now depreciated equipment, her home and her retirement.

There are two key concepts to take away from this sad tale. First, it's relatively easy to get that lump sum from the bank and forget that not only is it not your money, but you're paying money to borrow that money. Second, SBA loans can be brutal if you miss even one payment, because the laws allow the SBA and the banks to see you as a single entity with your business, regardless of legal set up in an LLC or Corporation. The Limited Liability part only goes so far because they require you to sign personally as well. There are other bank loans that also do the same thing.

CAN YOU START DEBT-FREE?

Loans to start a business are a little on the crazy side. Think about it. You don't have a product that you are selling yet. You don't have assets yet. You don't have financial statements because you haven't done anything yet, but you want somebody to give you money. You're guessing on how much you'll sell, how much you'll profit, how much your costs will be, and how fast you'll be able to pay back the money someone gives you on the strength of those guesses. That's a lot of guessing, but somehow, this has become the normal view of starting and funding a business. It's a high-risk environment and no investor (including a bank) is going to take it lightly, it will cost you in interest.

Different kinds of businesses have different requirements for startup and operations. It's not that you have to start off completely debt-free and without any loans; it's that any loans you consider taking must make absolute sense for your business. Let me repeat: you must be able to rid yourself of that debt as quickly as possible.

Some businesses will need capital improvements right away, and some of them will be more negotiable than others—a new bowling alley might need to lease a building, put in lanes, and purchase pin setting equipment and bowling balls right away. A CPA will need a computer and to have already taken care of his or her education and licensing. A manufacturing business might need one or more pieces of specialized equipment, and many of those kinds of machines may cost $100,000. Most small business owners don't have that kind of money in the bank and will feel the need to borrow. But taking even the most educated guess means you will lower your business's odds of success by endeavoring not to default on those loans. The risk is two sided.

STARTING UP SLOW AND SMALL

I recommend saving up your funds, starting as small as is practically possible, and then build up your company from there. There are many kinds of companies you can start with almost no money—Dan Miller even wrote an eBook called, *48 Low or No Cost Business Ideas*.

Sometimes you might feel that you have a limited time offer for a business opportunity, and don't have time to save up. For instance, several years ago a friend of mine came to me and said, "There's a flower store and gift shop for sale now in a very small community I like, and I'm going to borrow $150,000 to buy the store."

"Okay, that's fine," I told her, "but you really need to consider all the risks, find all the pros and cons on the equation. If you buy the store and all the merchandise in it, what is the likelihood of selling the inventory in your very, very small community? How long have they been holding the inventory? Who's your competition? Who else is selling the same things? Are people going to drive 75 miles one way to the big stores in the city to get better deals than what you can offer? How are you going to actually service that loan from your projected sales?"

Her response, "You know, I'm 45 years old and I'm going to do this for the next 30 years." In her situation, the things to consider included looking at the life of the loan and what it meant for her operating costs. If she took out $150,000 in loans, over 30 years she projects payments to be approximately $800 a month. Now she knows she must make $800 every month to service the loan, besides making enough for her other operating costs. She had to decide she wasn't going to stumble along for 30 years and instead was going to have to make extra money to pay the loan down. She had to look at the historical sales figures for the store and determine if they would allow her to pay off that loan with that inventory and future inventory and still comfortably make enough to cover her bills, payroll...**and pay herself**.

Another client told me they wanted to open a retail store, and they wanted to go to the bank for a loan to buy inventory. What if that inventory doesn't sell? Clearly, you'd better have a very good handle on your market to make some very good educated guesses on what to buy. You'll need to have a plan in place if the sales do not materialize. If the loan is to buy displays, clothing racks, and shelving, or for remodeling or other capital improvements, you need to know that those things depreciate very, very quickly and plan accordingly.

A START UP MINDSET

I've noticed a very interesting mindset that accompanies a large loan vs. when people are spending their saved funds to start up their companies.

When people get a sizable loan, it feels like free money. They'll take that $100,000 and spend it on brand new fixtures, an amazing lighting plan, fancy inventory systems, and other such improvements. All the money is quickly gone.

But when people are spending $20,000 that they've saved up, suddenly, every penny seems precious and they want to get as much bang for their buck as they can. Instead of getting the trendiest and latest of displays and mannequins, they'll check out other store closing sales listings and perhaps score a vintage look for their new space. They'll ask their brother-in-law to help them hang some shelves, or come up with a clever idea to make IKEA track curtains do double duty as backdrops to the store and changing rooms.

If we know we've invested $20,000 of our own money, we're more likely to take care of what we've bought, to be cleverer and more original with our purchases, and work harder to get that investment to work for us. We tend to pass that mentality on to our teams, employees, and anyone working with our company. Starting up with your own money means that you will almost automatically be more focused on what your business does with that money.

STARTING SMALLER = CONTROL

People assume that more is better when starting up, but if you look at case studies and listen to people's anecdotes, that's not true. When you start off bigger by buying more debt, it makes you less nimble and able to keep up with shifts your new business needs.

Frankly, retail (as an example) is a particularly brutal business, and you'll want to be able to switch directions on a dime, because the early bird gets that worm. If you have a business loan, the bank will be checking in with you periodically, they will want to see you sticking to the business plan that they made the loan on. If you discover that what your community really needs and wants is Halloween costumes when you originally thought they'd want high tech business toys, you're going to be stuck with a business plan that is built around those high-tech business toys until you can convince the bank to make the switch.

The loan means that you're now limited as to what you can do with your business, because you're now not the only person with say in how you run your business. Your loan agreement generally provides that the bank can shut down your business and call in the loan. The contract is the way they protect their money that they loan you, which is why the contracts are typically 20-30 pages, each of which you will want to read (yes, READ) and sign off on before taking the loan.

The same is true when you bring in a business partner. Yes, they usually bring an influx of funds, but you will also lose whatever percentage of control you've given them. Bob's BBQ Joint was doing well, and he decided he wanted to try some new sauce recipes on new meats, so he cooked some new things up and put them up on a specials board. His new business partner walked in the door and immediately said, "Wait, what's this? We didn't discuss this, what are you doing?"

The bottom line is that while they can bring cash, partnerships and banks can be somewhat problematic in terms of bringing in needed funds, because you'll also lose control over your business.

OPTIONS FOR FUNDING YOUR BUSINESS

FUNDING YOUR BUSINESS, YOURSELF

My most recommended method is to save up the money you need to start or upgrade your business. It gives you the most control, creates the most buy-in for you in your business, and has all the advantages we discussed.

BANK LOANS

There are several kinds of bank loans. In business, the one you hear most often is the SBA Business Loan, backed by the Small Business Administration. Depending on who you're talking to, the SBA loan is the best thing that ever happened to them or the worst. When it's the best thing, it's usually because they paid as agreed or paid it off early. It was a good short-term fix. When it's the worst thing, it's generally because missing a payment with an SBA meant they raised the interest rate or called in the loan. That loan's contract will attach all the assets of business, all the receivables, all the cash, and calls for a personal guarantee, so it's doubly important not to commingle your personal and business money with this loan type. You are personally liable for the loan and the SBA and the bank does not see a separation between you and your business, even if you file as an S Corp, LLP or LLC. An SBA loan puts you right back together again. (Some non-SBA bank loans will do that as well.)

PERSONAL LOANS

You may get a personal loan from your bank (often more easily than a business loan), put the money into your business, and call it a business loan from you personally. That is combining personal with business and it is risky because the business can go out of business, but you are still personally liable for that loan.

There's also personal loans from investing entities (such as angel investors), or from friends and family. Be sure to read the contracts on the former very carefully before signing so you know your liabilities. It's also important to remember that personal loans from friends and family are not governed by the laws of the FDIC or any other federal banking rules. If you're going to the Bank of Mom or Dad, it's very common that the parameters aren't laid out very well.

The risk on personal loans is, almost always, the relationship with that person. This kind of loan commonly comes from mom or dad's retirement money, which they're counting on having later in life. They're doing a favor for their child, but what they've done is risked their own retirement. If the business fails, you've sabotaged their retirement. Be sure both parties are comfortable with this risk.

If you have decided the risk is OK, then have a contract, even if it is Bank of Mom or Dad. This helps everyone have a clear understanding of the parameters of the loan. And, it will keep potential disagreements at bay with siblings.

CREDIT CARDS

When you get cash or other goods by using a credit card, you are buying a loan and using debt. This kind of loan is typically lower risk and unsecured, but a much higher interest rate. The credit card company will not micro-manage you or your business, but this method of getting funds is not ideal.

The interest rates are usually very high and the debt adds up quickly. Even if the card starts with a zero balance, after the "grace period" those rates can jump to 14-29% or higher before you get around to paying off the balance. Every time you use your credit card, you should have the money in the cash account, planned in the budget, planned in the cash flow, and you can use that money to pay off that credit card tomorrow.

Having a credit card to make online purchases and travel expenses makes sense, as all those things are now mainly purchased online. In fact, I would highly caution you against using a debit card for those transactions.

Your debit card is attached to your cash; if you rent a car then the rental company will put a $500 hold on the card (they do this in case you crash the car or steal it, etc.), and until that hold is lifted, you cannot use those funds. Hotels do the same thing. This can make life inconvenient.

The debit card normally carries the same "safety net" against fraud. I was working for a company several years ago that had direct pay with the hotel where I stayed. Management changed and someone had forgotten to tell the new staff that I wasn't responsible for my room. One day, they decided to run three full weeks' worth of hotel stays on my debit card. It wasn't fraud, it was a misunderstanding and it took me four days to get my money back into my account. If I was depending on that money for food or other payments, it could have been a huge problem.

Another risk of using debit cards, rather than credit cards, is the risk of fraud and identity theft. Fraud is very common now, and credit cards don't allow cyber thieves to touch your cash funds. Again, it can take days to get your money back into your bank account if they are trying to prove it's not fraud.

If you prefer to use debit cards for purchases like these because you don't want to incur debt, I would have a bank account specifically for that debit card's transactions only.

APR AND PRINCIPAL

When we sign up for debt or to get return on our investment, there's a percentage number called the APR: Annual Percentage Rate. This number describes your finance charge as an interest rate for an entire year, rather than describing a monthly rate or fee. Calculations of APR can be complicated, but when your bank loans you money, the bank will give you the APR based on all fees and costs, which is their margin (their profit) on your loan.

The bank advertises a loan with a fixed interest rate of 5.9%, but in order to calculate the APR from your vantage point you need to include fees like, origination fees and possible daily compounding. The total APR might end up being well above that advertised 5.9%.

That APR is coming directly from your bottom line, so I highly recommend that you pay loans as fast as possible. Remember to make those extra payments as *principal contribution*, otherwise, the bank will simply hold the funds you give them until the due date and state that you've made a payment on time, counting that payment as a future regular payment, not a payment towards principal. When you make a payment toward principal, you accelerate the term of the loan and can realize large savings in interest payments. If you notice your account is paid up through a later date you will know that the payments were applied to future payments instead of principal.

GROWING YOUR COMPANY

Knowing when to begin growing your company is a matter of understanding your cash flow. We have covered cash flow issues in other chapters, but remember that the most risk-averse method of starting up your company is to have other income coming in—working a job and using that money to fund your personal life, including starting up your own business, is the very best way if you can swing that. That can work for growth as well.

Growth plans are another great reason to become debt-free as quickly as possible, because the more funds you can put into your business or opportunity savings (or Sinking Funds), the better. When you are always chasing your debt payments, there's less money for the saving funds.

As we discussed in other chapters, always squirrel money away for your emergency fund first, then fund your account for purchases you know are coming and then concentrate on becoming debt free.

Once you are debt-free, the single most pressing area that most small business owners want to grow in is usually the variety of their inventory or product. It's important to really sit down and make sure that what you want to bring in, is what your customers actually want. My clients will say to me, "I need more stuff, my customers want more variety." Be very sure that they want variety. Big block stores can carry many brands and varieties of the same item, but most people already know what brands they want to buy. Look at successful businesses roughly the same size as your own business. How do they stock? Do they have many colors and sizes of the same items? Do they have a lot of different items, different styles, or a wide variety of items?

Christopher Banks, for instance, is a great store model for medium-sized retailers of clothing. They don't carry that many items, but they'll have perhaps four or five of the latest colorways in each item, and of course multiple sizes. They do not have extreme levels of variety.

A client of mine is a buyer for a major lingerie chain. She can tell you exactly what sizes and what colors of what models that each store in the chain needs to have, based on the sales figures history and projections. This national chain has enough funding to be able to have many different models of each kind of lingerie, but even they limit themselves. Be as sure as you can that how you expand your lines is what your customers will actually buy.

GETTING OUT OF DEBT AND THE "WRITE-OFF"

So, what if you've started this book after already starting your company with debt. Don't worry, that just makes you normal. I like to think of truly successful business owners as not normal. All you should do is what we did, change your mindset about debt. Stop making it a part of your life and stop signing those loan papers and buying that sort of product.

When we were staring at $500,000 in debt in 2001, it was overwhelming at the first glance. Our first thoughts were, "Well, now we've done it, we'll never get out of this mess." Then, we buckled down. We defined Needs vs. Wants in our personal lives and in our business. Defining our needs vs. wants allowed us to prioritize our money and stress less about bringing in as much money from the business.

One of the first things we learned to do was walk away from the mindset of the word "write-off". I hear this term daily. Until we really learned what the word does against us, it was a part of our lives. We'd buy things we didn't need because we could "write it off from our taxes." That implies that if I spend $1,000, I save $1,000 in taxes. When

I ask my clients if they understand the term, they come up with the same answer. It wasn't until my wonderful CPA sat us down and showed us that there is really no such thing as a "write-off" the way everyone uses the term. The only way you can get a true "write-off" is with tax credits. A tax credit is dollar for dollar savings. Everything else is a business expense or a deduction.

The deduction works like this—buy something for $1,000 and you can deduct in the form of an expense which is subtracted from your income to lower your profit. That deduction will lower taxes by your tax rate. So, if you are taxed at a rate of 30% then effectively you have spent $1,000 to save $300 in taxes. Now, like you, I don't like to pay any more in taxes than I must. But, this is a recipe for disaster to buy something for $1,000 (that I might not need or doesn't really help my business) in order to stop sending $300 to the government.

Next time you say "write off" ask yourself, "Is this an expense I need that will help my business run more smoothly or bring in more customers?" If they answer is "yes", then go for it; if the answer is "no", stop and save yourself some money.

THE DEBT ELIMINATION SNOWBALL!

This is my favorite lesson I learned from Dave Ramsey. The Debt Elimination Snowball is the simplest solution to getting out of debt. It's not a magic formula, but it is a formula that works.

It's simple. List all your debts, smallest balance to largest balance. List all your minimum payments. Then, regardless of interest rate, go attack that smallest debt with everything you've got. Get rid of it FAST. Try to eliminate it in the 1st month of you reading this book. Recently, there was a study done that said that most American's are more concerned with eliminating debt than they are with investing. Here it is folks. Do it!

Then, after you have eliminated that first debt, take whatever payment you were making towards it, and start attacking the next debt in the list, when that's gone, do the same with the next debt. This is the snowball effect (think snowman). Each time you eliminate a debt you add that payment to the next debt and you are building momentum. I've run this math for multiple clients, when you see it on paper that your debt snowball is going to take less than 5-7 years (ours was huge and took 7 ½ years) you will say, "WOW, I'm starting this today!"

REVIEW BOB'S BBQ JOINT'S DEBT ELIMINATION CHART

You can see that based on the budget that Bob's BBQ will be able to add an additional $975 per month towards the company's debt. If he can do that consistently, the company will be debt free in 5-7 years when using the Debt Elimination Calculator. Even if he misses a month he'll still be on track to be debt free.

DEBT ELIMINATION CALCULATOR				
	Amount Available	Min Total	Remaining to Allocate	
Payment Budget:	$1,500.00	$525.00	$975.00	
Unique Debt Name	Total Payoff	Minimum Payment	Extra Payment	Payments Remaning at Minimum
Credit Card - Old	$ 500.00	$ 25.00	$ 475.00	1
Bank Loan - 1st Bank	$ 3,911.32	$ 100.00	$ 500.00	7
Credit Card - Personal	$ 5,000.00	$ 50.00	$ -	100
Bank Loan - Credit Union	$ 10,000.00	$ 150.00	$ -	67
Vehicle Loan	$ 33,682.65	$ 200.00	$ -	168
Operating Loan	$ 40,000.00	$ -	$ -	?
TOTAL	$ 93,094.00	$ 525.00	$ 975.00	
62.1 Payments Remaining at Available Amount				

THE GIFT THAT KEEPS ON GIVING

That freedom from debt is the gift that keeps on giving. It works personally and in your business. It drives your opportunities for growth, your opportunities to expand, to acquire other companies, or lines of business increase dramatically when you are not servicing debt. Think carefully about what you need to fund your startup, or what you need to grow your business. It is highly likely that you can make do with less than you originally believed and give yourself much more opportunity for growth and success.

Use the template below to help get started on your Debt Snowball (you can also download the spreadsheet at RockinYourBusinessFinances.com).

DEBT ELIMINATION CALCULATOR				
	Amount Available	Min Total	Remaining to Allocate	
Payment Budget:				
Unique Debt Name	Total Payoff	Minimum Payment	Extra Payment	Payments Remaning at Minimum
TOTAL				

IT'S YOUR TURN

If you are starting a business, how do you plan to fund it?

_____

_____

_____

_____

_____

What other options for funding exist?

_____

_____

_____

_____

_____

If your business is currently operating, what debt do you have now? Don't be afraid to go and add up the numbers.

_____

_____

_____

_____

_____

What can you do differently to start and operate debt free?

_____

_____

_____

_____

_____

_____

What will it take for you to make a commitment to operate debt free?

_____

_____

_____

_____

_____

_____

What is your #1 question about operating your business 100% DEBT FREE?

How Many Months—using the Debt Elimination Calculator—will it take you to be DEBT FREE?

HELP Motivate Others—Share your answers online at RockinYourBusinessFinances.com and enter to win a free hour of Small Biz Coaching.

CHAPTER 7
SAFETY NET

It's time to examine emergency funds and short-term savings funds more closely. These are vitally important funds, and can easily be the difference between the success, or the failure of your business.

EMERGENCY FUNDS

When emergencies happen, I hear the same things repeatedly: "I have my credit card for an emergency," or, "I'll get a line of credit at the bank for an emergency." The reality is that we should plan for emergencies, because we know they're coming, we just don't know when. Like death and taxes, the other thing that's certain about life is that it's uncertain. The bank knows that emergencies are coming, that's why they sell you those great debt products for emergencies!

In a true emergency, do you really want to add another debt to the bank—adding more strain to your business? Or would you rather have the funds set aside so that if something happens you can just pay for it and move on?

Other than having funds in this account, the next most important thing is that this account must be separate from your day-to-day operating account, or it becomes the "BBD" money (Bigger, Better, Deal). It is not to be used for a newer piece of equipment, a case lot sale, or even "I need a car to wrap to advertise my business". It should be at a different bank to keep the ease of just transferring back and forth from happening in short-term cash flow problems. You must define what an emergency is in your business. For example, for Bob's BBQ Joint, an emergency is a fire in the building and having to close the doors for repairs. The insurance pays for the building, but the emergency fund can keep the staff from being suddenly unemployed. It can pay for a vital piece of equipment when it breaks (although these things break and could be saved for in advance). It could be to help in the case of a natural disaster to help keep your bills paid and your staff from the poor house.

An emergency fund means that you don't have to say, "The client forgot to pay me, so you're laid off, sorry," to your team. It means that the bad thing that happens doesn't cause a drop-dead emergency for your company and forces you to close the doors.

Maybe you are in sales and you must have a car to cover your territory and your car catastrophically breaks down with needs for a major repair (now you also need a rental car). Perhaps clients didn't pay as promised, you can't make the rent, and now the leasing agent is threatening to kick you out of your office. You're in manufacturing and a key part snaps in two, and you must send it off to Switzerland for a replacement part. This part must be sent overnight international shipping, or you'll have to send everyone on the line home.

You need to know what an emergency truly is. It's not for short term cash flow issues—that's not an emergency. You should be looking at that in your cash flow plans by allowing for up to two weeks of cash flow problems, however, if it goes for over two or three weeks it'll affect your payroll, and that might be defined as a short-term emergency fix.

And, of course, once you've dipped into your emergency fund, you need to build that fund back up for the next unforeseen problem, as soon as possible.

How much you have in your emergency fund will depend on your business. What I generally recommend is to gather three months of your Four Walls expenses for a good beginning point for your emergency fund target. We've talked about the Four Walls of your business, the things that your business absolutely will not be able to function without, make sure you have at least that amount in your emergency fund to cover you for three months.

Start with one month's worth and work up. Six months to a year of Four Walls expenses is your true goal once your business is past the start-up phase. The amount could be a few thousand, or, if you're a company with a payroll that must be covered, it might be $100k or more.

Lastly, **do not invest** with your emergency funds. Those funds are at a certain amount for good reason, and as soon as you invest you're inviting chaos into your life to create havoc, and you may lose some of your money to the market.

FACTORING

This is somewhat of a new concept we should discuss. An "investor" will buy your receivables. You're expecting a check from a client for $40,000, the investor will buy that receivable from you, give you $30,000 in cash, and when the $40,000 comes in, he'll keep the $40,000, paying off your $30,000 and giving him a profit of $10,000—25% to the Factor.

That isn't just a good return on investment for the investor, that's a screaming return on investment. There's risk that the receivable never gets paid, but for the most part, it's not that much risk. He's just betting on your poor planning and that you haven't set money aside for that 30-60 days.

When I first heard about these businesses, my immediate reaction was, "Do people actually sign up for this?" It's a pure sign of not knowing your numbers. You sold your product, your $40,000 worth of product, but because you haven't taken the time to realize that you have cash flow drops in your business, you're going to sell 100%—or more—of that *profit* to this investor. You're managing your cash on a "fly by the seat of your pants" basis.

This is similar to a "business line of credit." Banks offer you a $40,000 line of credit. You say to yourself, "We'll never use it all, don't worry. Maybe $5,000 here or there.

We got the big number just as a safety net." Usually within less than a year, the line of credit has been eaten up, plus credit cards, and generally you still haven't said, "Here's my cash and this is what I need to function on." The line of credit keeps you from knowing your numbers and you use that line of credit like it was income.

Realize that what you're doing is buying a product. Then you can make a good decision about whether you want to buy that product. I often hear small business owners say something like, "I went and asked the bank if they would help me, it was just a short-term issue." You're begging them to sell you their product to you. Do you have your clients begging you to sell your product to them?

SHORT TERM SAVINGS FUNDS, AKA "THE SINK"

This one financial tool is probably more important than all the other tools in this workbook. If you can work the Sinking Fund as it is meant, then you can say goodbye to most of your financial woes.

There are several different kinds of funds that fall under the heading of "short-term." Most of them are part of the "sinking fund." A Sinking Fund is an old accounting term for money that you save "into the sink" for all the expenses you know will be coming up, regular maintenance work for the sales professional's car, a new oven at Bob's BBQ Joint, the months when you know business will be slow, or finding that bigger, better deal (the BBD) on something you know you'll 'need'.

You will definitely want to separate the emergency fund from the Sinking Fund. The best scenario is that you've planned your cash flow and upcoming expenses so well that your emergency fund simply sits there, like the airbags in a car. But when you really need it, the air bags are there to save you. The short-term savings you plan on using are there and it keeps you from dipping into your emergency fund for things you know are coming. And, for things that are not truly emergencies.

To start, figure out what annual or quarterly expenses come up throughout the year: business insurance (this can be an annual expense), car insurance (quarterly or bi-annually), or a new stove for Bob's BBQ Joint. Figure out how much those items are on an annual basis and divide by 12—now you have a monthly "payment" amount for your Sinking Fund. You will see this account grow and see that now those events can happen and it won't crash your cash flow, you will just go to the Sinking Fund to pay for your annual insurance.

Keep this account organized. You will want to know that $10,000 is to be broken up for things you know are coming—$1,000 for car repair, $4,000 for insurance, $5,000 for that new stove. I recommend you simply keep a spreadsheet with all the upcoming expenses. This will also keep you from thinking, "Hey, $10k in the account I can go buy something." The spreadsheet will keep you focused. Keep in mind that you can reallocate the money in your Sinking Fund as needs come up, so long as you keep track of everything. Sometimes being able to shift funds easily is not a bad way to go— especially if you find that new stove for $2,500 instead of $5,000.

If you're not organized and you know you'll likely dip from one category to make up for a shortfall in another category, you might want to separate the different funds out into different accounts. Many banks will do this for you. They will also help you create an automatic transaction to help you stay on track.

Let's see what happened with Bob's BBQ Joint. Bob knew he would need a new delivery van soon. The vehicle he has scoped out was a $54,000 van. Bob started saving a few years ago by putting $800/month into his Sinking Fund (about the same amount as a normal van/truck payment). One day he was just surfing the internet to see if another brand van with similar features was on the market. He was in luck; for $46,000 he could buy a different model with better features. That is a BBD and it makes sense to buy now, correct?

So, Bob went to his spreadsheet to see where he was in his account. He has $58,000 in that account. He's realizing that he only has $38,000 of that saved for the van. On his spreadsheet, he sees that he also has $5,000 in his Sinking Fund that's set aside for next Christmas's employee awards party. And, $5,000 for the stove (the old one is still working fine), and his annual insurance payment is coming up for $10,000. Bob does the math—If he can negotiate the price of the van down to $43,000, because he's doing a cash deal, then he can temporarily move some of the new stove money and some of the employee bonus money to the van account. Now he can buy the van and continue to make the normal $800 to the Sinking Fund to replenish the stove and bonus accounts before they are needed. Since he will no longer be saving for the van, Bob decides to purchase the BBD and reallocate the Sinking Fund.

Sinking Funds are how you save for equipment you know will need to be replaced: a new computer, that newer vehicle, new shop equipment to replace old, or perhaps maintenance funds to keep older equipment running well so you don't have to replace them as often.

Property tax is another upcoming expense for which you should be setting aside funds. Your annual Christmas party, end of year bonus, ongoing education, a new roof for the building; all are perfect examples to put into the SINK to keep business out of debt.

HOW TO GET STARTED

Getting started is not scary or difficult. Go and open a savings account now—the scariest part is not getting started! Start putting money in it every month (a payment to yourself), even if it's just $100. You should treat this as if you've taken out a loan, a non-negotiable payment to yourself for the health of your business. A $500 payment to yourself over 60 months = $30,000 + interest is not the same as taking out a $30,000 loan for 60 months @ 6%, your payment = $580.00, for a total of $34,800 over the course of the loan.

I'm often asked, "What if I have more than one thing I need to be saving for? Should I be making one big payment, or split that into four payments for four different things?" I make one payment that is the total of all things and then separate the items on my spreadsheet. Remember, the KISS method, the simple way is always going to be easier. It will also be habit forming, I find myself upping the amount periodically, because as my sales increase so will my need for replacing things.

Determine the amount that you need to be paying into the Sinking Fund and set it up as an automatic payment as you would for a bank loan. Make it Non-Negotiable and part of your Four Walls! You will be amazed at how quickly your Sinking Fund savings will start to grow.

Probably one of the most amazing things I see happen to folks when they effectively start using their Sinking Fund, is that you become much more conscious of your money and how you want to spend it. You will start negotiating insurance rates and purchase price of things, and being much more focused on how you spend your hard, earned dollars.

You may reach a certain point and realize that you want to re-prioritize where you want to spend that money, and that's fine. The point is that now you can do that, whereas, before, you would have had to borrow that money. And if you spend that money in a smart way, by investing in things that save you money in labor costs or other overhead, you take those savings and put it into the Sinking Fund to start building that up for other goals.

You can also take new sources of money and put those into your Sinking Fund instead of spending it right away. Bob's BBQ Joint got a catering job that took him out of his normal area, the company agreed to pay mileage in addition to his normal delivery fee. He kept those funds separate from his normal operating budget, other than paying for gas to that job. He took the rest and added it to his new van Sinking Fund. Just that little move put his Sinking Fund higher sooner so he could get that great deal on his new van.

The longer you do these things, the more money and cash flow you'll have working for you. And, the more it becomes a good habit, like brushing your teeth.

BOB's BBQ - SINKING FUND ALLOCATION

Instructions: Enter Dates, Deposits, & Withdrawals.

| | Account | | | | Non-monthly Expenses & Emergency Fund | | | | | | | | | |
| | | | | | Assign a portion of the balance to these categories | | | | | | | | | |
Date	Deposit	Withdrawal	Current Balance	Remaining To Allocate	Emergency	Bonus / Christmas	New Delivery VAN	New Stove	Slow Month	Slow Month	Slow Month	Slow Month	Next New Delivery Van	Misc Other
			Goal Amounts:		$ 25,000.00	$ 5,000.00	$ 43,000.00	$ 5,000.00	$ 4,000.00	$ 4,000.00	$ 4,000.00	$ 4,000.00	$ 40,000.00	$ 10,000.00
	Starting Balance:		$ 40,000.00	$ -	$ 10,000.00	$ 5,000.00	$ 20,000.00	$ 5,000.00						
1-Jan	$ 1,000.00	$ -	$ 41,000.00	$ -			$ 1,000.00							
1-Feb	$ 1,000.00	$ -	$ 42,000.00	$ -			$ 1,000.00							
1-Mar	$ 3,000.00	$ -	$ 45,000.00	$ -			$ 3,000.00							
1-Apr	$ 3,000.00	$ -	$ 48,000.00	$ -			$ 3,000.00							
1-May	$ 10,000.00	$ -	$ 58,000.00	$ -			$ 6,000.00		$ 4,000.00					
1-Jun	$ 4,000.00	$ -	$ 62,000.00	$ -			$ 4,000.00							
1-Jul	$ 4,000.00	$ -	$ 66,000.00	$ -		$ (2,500.00)	$ 5,000.00	$ (2,500.00)		$ 4,000.00				
1-Aug	$ 5,000.00	$ 43,000.00	$ 28,000.00	$ -		$ 1,000.00	$ (43,000.00)	$ 1,000.00			$ 3,000.00			
1-Sep	$ 6,000.00	$ -	$ 34,000.00	$ -	$ 1,000.00	$ 1,000.00		$ 1,000.00				$ 1,000.00	$ 500.00	$ 1,500.00
1-Oct	$ 3,000.00	$ -	$ 37,000.00	$ -		$ 500.00		$ 500.00					$ 500.00	$ 1,500.00
1-Nov	$ 1,000.00	$ -	$ 38,000.00	$ -	$ 1,000.00									
1-Dec	$ 10,000.00	$ -	$ 48,000.00	$ -	$ 5,000.00									$ 5,000.00
1-Jan	$ -	$ -	$ 48,000.00	$ -										
1-Feb	$ -	$ -	$ 48,000.00	$ -										
1-Mar	$ -	$ -	$ 48,000.00	$ -										
			Total saved for each category:		$ 17,000.00	$ 5,000.00	$ -	$ 5,000.00	$ 4,000.00	$ 4,000.00	$ 4,000.00	$ 4,000.00	$ 1,000.00	$ 8,000.00

Total Budgeted (all categories): $48,000.00

- SINKING FUND ALLOCATION

Account

Instructions: Enter Dates, Deposits, & Withdrawals

Date	Deposit	Withdrawal	Current Balance	Remaining To Allocate
			Goal Amounts:	
		Starting Balance:	$.	$.
today			$.	$.
			Total saved for each category:	

Non-monthly Expenses & Emergency Fund

Assign a portion of the balance to these categories

$.	$.	$.	$.	$.	$.	$.	$.	$.	$.
$.	$.	$.	$.	$.	$.	$.	$.	$.	$.
$.	$.	$.	$.	$.	$.	$.	$.	$.	$.

Total Budgeted (all categories): $0.00

IT'S YOUR TURN

Define an Emergency in YOUR Business.

_____

_____

_____

_____

Do you have an emergency fund in place? How much?

_____

_____

How many months of Four Walls expenses does it represent?

_____

_____

_____

_____

If you don't have one, start NOW! How much can you start that fund with?

_____

_____

_____

_____

How much per month will you put into the fund?

_____

_____

_____

How long will it take to get one month worth of Four Walls expenses built up?

_____

_____

_____

What items in your business would benefit from a Sinking Fund account?

_____

_____

_____

_____

_____

Which items in your budget belong in the Sinking Fund?

_____

_____

_____

_____

_____

Starting now, how much is your new payment to yourself?

_____

_____

_____

_____

_____

Are you feeling the added benefit of Defining Your Business Savings?

_____

_____

_____

_____

_____

For FREE Spreadsheets and Forms,
visit RockinYourBusinessFinances.com.

CHAPTER 8
CREATING BENEFITS

BENEFITS! I can't tell you how often I meet with people who won't leave the job they hate because of the "benefits!" When starting your own business creating your OWN benefits must be a part of that plan. Remember when we talked about having a "tax" mentality? A business can legally and legitimately create its own benefits plan for its employees, even if you are the only employee.

When Bob's BBQ Joint first started, Bob was young and had a fabulous recipe for the best BBQ ever! Bob didn't come from a family of business owners—he started from scratch. In the beginning, it was a recipe and a makeshift building and a dream. He had no employees for quite a while, just himself. So, you can imagine starting out Bob had to be chef, dishwasher, cashier, ordering/inventory, bookkeeper, and then some in his business.

At what point, did someone pull him aside to teach him how to run his business? At what point, was he reading tax documents to understand what he could do to lessen his tax liabilities? At what point, was he going to sit down and learn what benefits to create for himself?

It's completely understandable that he was out making amazing BBQ not thinking about having a tax mentality, but how long do *you* wish to not take advantage of the many ways the government has given small business owners a break in tax liabilities?

WHY BENEFITS OVER PAYCHECKS?

Most working people have a job for income and the benefits. The obvious benefit is your hourly wage or salary. Other benefits will depend upon the company: retirement plans, health insurance, a company vehicle, cell phones, gym memberships, etc.

When we interview for a position at a company, we look at the benefits provided to decide whether we want to work there. Is the salary fair? Does the company contribute to retirement plans? Does it further my career and/or education? Benefits are clearly important factors in our plans to decide which companies to work for, whenever we work for anyone else.

But when people start up their own companies, suddenly the benefits go out the window. This is the opposite of the way we usually select our employer. We treat ourselves worse than we expect an employer to treat us! So many business owners pay themselves under a subsistence level and wait on any benefits until "later."

Why would you or anyone else work for a company that only pays you a subsistence-level wage with little to no other benefits? If you wouldn't work for another company paying you at that level, you might want to reconsider running a company that cannot provide benefits. We're back to whether you have a business or an over-grown hobby.

The overall idea of leaving our jobs to create a business we love and that will replace our income is vastly misunderstood. Remember the chart Making More by Making Less (if you've bounced around—yes, I did just say that—go back to Chapter 5 to refresh your memory).

If our businesses can create a benefits plan for our employees, then it can also create a benefits plan for the owner of the company. Many things you pay for in your day-to-day life can legally and legitimately be paid for by the company.

Several years ago, I had one of those funky paycheck moments when my actual paycheck, my take home pay, was only $107. For those of you reading this book, you are thinking—that's it, she's crazy. Did she just "brag" about paying herself $107? I am reading this as I write and wondering if I should include this in my book. That is because, "what professional business coach would brag about a paycheck for $107?"

In reality, it wasn't a $107 paycheck. Because I have a tax mentality, my gross for the pay period was 50% of profit or $5,000, (my overall profit was $10,000 for that pay period) to keep in line with IRS reasonable wage guidelines. Then, I fully funded my SIMPLE IRA for that period (in this case it was $3,150; and my company matched at 3%). Knowing my overall profit for my business for this pay period, I added extra tax payments to federal/state withholding to compensate for the draw I'd take that wasn't on payroll. After I deducted all that was legal and legitimate for a pay period, my actual paycheck was $107. As a business owner, I could (and would) take additional funds in draw format to bring money home to my household. Additionally, I paid the extra tax in the paycheck to avoid having to pay additional quarterly estimates (if you don't pay enough tax in payroll the IRS could require quarterly estimated taxes).

Remember, you must pay taxes (including FICA) on your paychecks, but you do not pay taxes on expenses and benefits. Expenses need to be legal and legitimate, as well as reasonable. You can expense your smart phone, but you can't expense smart phones for 4 kids in your family, unless, of course, they work for your company and need those phones as part of their jobs. Benefits must be reasonable as well, but there is a lot of room to create benefits in a company you'd love to work for if it wasn't already yours.

In this chapter, we're going to talk about retirement, a biggie, and in Chapter 9 we will talk about other benefits available to small businesses. Let's get started with creating retirement benefits. I'm not going to go too far into specifics as some of these change, but let's talk about at least a general, conceptual level of the retirement benefit building process.

RETIREMENT BENEFITS

When people are nervous about leaving a job to start their own companies, it's often because of the retirement benefits, especially the matching funds for 401(k) plans. You can still have that benefit when you are a small business.

There are three plans that I generally recommend for most companies, SIMPLE IRA, SEP-IRA, and Individual 401(k). The following information is based on material that is currently available.

SIMPLE IRA (THIS IS MY FAVORITE)

A SIMPLE IRA plan is a Savings Incentive Match Plan for Employees. It gives small employers a simplified method to make contributions toward their employees' retirement and their own retirement.

According to the IRS, under a SIMPLE IRA plan, an employer can contribute each year one of two ways: matching employee contributions up to 3% of compensation or contribute 2% non-elective contribution for each eligible employee. With the 2% non-elective contribution, even if the employee does not contribute to his or her SIMPLE IRA, the employer must still contribute equal to 2% of the employee's compensation up to the annual limit of $255,000, as of 2013.

SIMPLE IRAs, are just that simple—easy to set up and easy to manage. As of 2017, an individual may contribute $12,500 per year as an employee, including yourself. If the employee is over 50, they may contribute an additional $3,000 as a makeup contribution into that plan, which comes out of their pre-tax salary. If they don't contribute, you don't have to match any funds.

I recommend that you match to the maximum amount: 3%. Regardless of how much someone contributes, the company can only match up to 3%. What the company matches for you must be the same as what they match for any other employees.

The SIMPLE IRA is easy if you have a small team. Set-up is minimal. The fees are super low, and you may self-direct it, or you can get a financial advisor to help you (which I recommend if you are not a financial expert).

SEP-IRA

A Simplified Employee Pension Plan (SEP) provides business owners with a simplified method to contribute toward their employees' as well as their own retirement savings. Contributions are made to an Individual Retirement Account (IRA) set up for each plan participant (a SEP-IRA).

A SEP-IRA account is a traditional IRA and follows the same investment, distribution, and rollover rules as traditional IRAs. The amount you can invest is convoluted, and you'll need to know your numbers, but it can be an excellent plan. It's based on your profit and a percentage of your profit, calculated backwards. The calculations can be rather complex, so you really should have a CPA for a SEP-IRA plan.

401(K)

A 401(k) is Section 401, subsection (k) in the tax code for qualified IRA and profit sharing plans that allows employees to contribute a portion of their wages to individual accounts. Elective salary deferrals are excluded from the employee's taxable income (except for designated 401(k) Roth deferrals). Employers can contribute to employees' accounts as a matching percentage and/or as profit sharing bonus.

You generally do not want to start up a 401(k) unless you have 50 employees or more, or unless it's one individual (just yourself) and you plan to keep it that way. It's expensive as a plan for a group of 2-49 employees. However, it can be very easy and, surprisingly, inexpensive for a single person. I do recommend having a financial advisor help you set this up.

POTENTIAL PROBLEMS

The IRS has some strict guidelines on retirement plans for companies and retirement plans within a household. I would always recommend you contact both your CPA and Financial Advisor to be sure you are meeting all the guidelines of the IRS rules. The last thing you want to have to do is go back and pay taxes on money you thought was deductible.

LONG TERM GOALS

If your long-term goals for your company are to be the only employee/owner, I would recommend either the SEP-IRA or the Single Person 401(k). If you are a single person operation but plan to have a team, then consider the SIMPLE IRA, it is very easy to add them to that plan, to navigate the payroll and bookkeeping sides, and to make the contributions.

The best thing about matching contributions, of course, is that you immediately have a 100% return on investment. There's nowhere else I know of that you can do that with such rapidity and assurance.

THE DETAILS

Be sure to double-check the latest rules for retirement benefits on the IRS.gov website and make sure your CPA is well versed on the rules as well. The IRS also has some very helpful checkup forms to help you review and find potential errors in your plans.

As you develop and implement your benefits package, be sure to add information to your business plan or to a benefits package document. Not only does this make it easy for you to find all the information about your benefits packages when you need them, but it makes it much easier during an audit to show the IRS that you had planned to provide your company's employee (yourself) benefits instead of trying to hide profit as your company has grown.

And, as always, stay on top of updating your paperwork as you plan, add, and change your benefits packages—and pat yourself on the back for creating a place you're happy to work!

IT'S YOUR TURN

You might have come up with a lot more questions than answers in this chapter. Write down as many questions as you can and contact an advisor.

_____

_____

_____

_____

_____

_____

_____

_____

Since you are getting a firm handle on your business finances, what are your next steps to providing your amazing benefits package?

_____

_____

_____

_____

_____

_____

_____

What retirement plan will be the best for your company and why?

_____

_____

_____

_____

_____

_____

_____

Will you need to cover only yourself, or do you have employees or plan to have employees in the future? How does that affect your decision making?

_____

_____

_____

_____

_____

_____

_____

**_For FREE Spreadsheets and Forms,
visit RockinYourBusinessFinances.com._**

CHAPTER 9
CREATING YOUR OWN BENEFITS

In the same way, you create a place where you're happy to work, do the same for your team. Offer them the same benefits package that you have yourself. If your team feels you really care about them, they'll do a better job. It's tempting to cut corners on benefits, but that's a shortcut with disadvantages that may not be immediately apparent.

When employees work for a company where the owner of a company gets all the benefits, all the stock options, all the profit, all the brand-new vehicles, all the health benefits, all the retirement benefits, and all they get is their hourly wage, do you think they believe the owner cares about them? When your employees believe you don't care about them, and something in their life needs to change, guess who gets the short end of the stick? You do, and it typically starts the cycle of looking for something better.

Statistics clearly illustrate that if you show that you care about your teammates, if they are part of your business family, you will have virtually no turnover. Your employees will work harder for you. They'll care more about your product. They'll help your company become successful because you are helping them be successful too!

I have a client whose industry historically has some of the lowest wages, but some of the most heart-wrenching work. The owner sees the direct benefit to his team and his company by offering stellar benefits and above-average wages for his team. The team sees this effort; and as a direct result his company has little to no turnover. And a team that works together for a common goal has exceptionally happy clients!

How much is that worth to the company? How do you measure it? In the book, *The Dream Manager*, Matthew Kelly says that, "70% of companies that offer a dream coach have virtually no turnover and 70% have better profits." They save the costs of low productivity, losing employees, and training new employees by providing benefits the team values. A company that is not fighting its own employees to get work done will have that much more energy to make themselves successful.

Maybe you want to be in business for yourself, but you're staying in your day job, because you don't want to lose your benefits. This is generally because most of us don't know how to create and how to afford benefits, not just for ourselves but for our potential employees.

Remember it's important, to keep your company separate from yourself. Even if you are a solo entrepreneur your company is its own thing, and you are the 1st teammate. As that first teammate, what benefits do you need to replace from your former job or what do you want to add for your team to help them succeed in life?

BENEFITS FOR YOU AND YOUR STAFF

Are you having a hard time personally paying your bills? Go down the list of your personal bills and see if any of them are benefits the company can offer you. When you are doing this, you need to keep this in mind: what would help you be better at your job if the company paid for it? Benefits work in multiple ways for your company. You can make your benefits be extremely rewarding for you and your employees. Again, it's wise to document the benefit package in your business plan, which can be very helpful to support your benefits to the IRS should you be audited.

Be intentional about your benefits. This goes back to the "write-off" mentality. We do not want to spend the business money on benefits that don't benefit the company or the team. For example, Google has a large team and has found that some basic wellness programs increase productivity of their team. So, there is little question about the benefits being a good investment for the company.

Some examples of benefits:

- Health and wellness benefits (health insurance premiums, workout classes, massages, gym memberships. This needs to be legal and legitimate for regular, non-sporadic visits. Many companies will reimburse with proof of participation at a gym)

- Vacation Pay

- Car allowance and mileage reimbursement

- Further education

- Some Meals & Training Events

- Paid time off

- Retirement (as noted in Chapter 8)

- Cell phone reimbursement

- Home office reimbursement

- Coaching or Counseling

- Even some clothing (this is a great way to get your team to wear your brand)

- Company parties or sponsored trips

This is part of making more by making less, as your business pays for more benefits, your bottom line goes down. Instead of making $70k profit, you make $50k, and things that you would be paying for personally is now being paid for by the company, so long as the benefits are legal and legitimate for operating businesses you now have a lower need to bring more money home. Because now the business is paying expenses that maybe you paid personally in the past.

It's the same for your team—what would help them be better at their job if the company paid for it as a benefit? What kind of benefits would reward both them and your company?

At Bob's BBQ Joint, Bob knows his wait staff are on their feet throughout their entire shift. He wants them in good health, because he knows he'll have fewer days when servers miss work due to illness. Servers who feel good will provide better service to his customers. A benefit at Bob's BBQ Joint is a bi-weekly massage; he pays a therapist come to the office to offer massages to his staff on their time off, Bob also benefits as he is also part of the staff.

Other benefits include on the job meals, paid leave (yes even for tipped wait staff), medical insurance and retirement. Since his team has fluctuating income from tips, he also has a Dream Coach that works with them each month to help them reach their own financial goals. Periodically he will hire a guest speaker to the staff meetings to help them grow as people within the organization. Of course, as the owner, he also participates in each of the benefits.

The direct result trickles down to his staff and returned to Bob when his team feels that Bob cares for them, and who they are as people not just what they bring to the company, it enhances loyalty to Bob's BBQ Joint. Bob's BBQ Joint could just be a summer or part-time job to his staff, but instead, they feel like family.

YOUR BOTTOM LINE

It's important to remember to include the costs of benefits for each person when setting your pricing, whether it's for you, your team, or for future employees. The rule of thumb is to triple the hourly rate if charging for labor. A laborer who gets paid $20 an hour will be charged to the customer at roughly $60 to pay for their benefits, taxes, and withholdings and make a profit.

For a $20 an hour employee, you'll add in 7.65% to pay your side of their Social Security and Medicare (FICA), plus workers' compensation insurance, overhead, uniforms, bonus, paid time off and tools, for instance. Then, if you're doing a SIMPLE IRA, add in up to 3% of the wages for your share of the employee's SIMPLE IRA, plus any additional benefits you want to provide as previously discussed. You'll also want to be sure you have included other required taxes, such as federal and state unemployment insurance (tax).

This almost always adds up to roughly double the wage to get to the break-even point. If you want to make money on your employee's labor costs, then you will have to raise the rate over that doubled rate.

On the plus side, when you're negotiating salary with your employees, you'll be able to point out that a salary of $15-20 an hour adds up to quite a bit more once they factor in the benefits. That can be a powerful tool for negotiating for good employees.

WHAT IS TAXABLE?

When you give a benefit to your employees, you must have those costs within your accounting software. Your accountant or bookkeeper will need to assign the benefit to the correct account in your chart of accounts. Some benefits are taxable, and some are not which impacts both your bottom line and the employee's. It's important to get it right.

The IRS rules state that cash or cash-equivalents are taxable to the employee—a $100 cash bonus or $200 gift card will need to be reflected on the employee's W-2. A health club membership should be paid by your company directly. Since it can't be used as cash, it does not fall under cash or cash-equivalent status.

If it's cash or can be used as cash, it goes on the paycheck. If the benefit is a non-cash gift, it doesn't have to go on the paycheck. If you give a gas card, is that a non-taxable gift of gas? No, because the gas card can be used in the convenience store for food, too. When it can be used for purchasing something, then it should be on the paycheck as taxable. A Christmas turkey is not a taxable benefit, because theoretically, you can't buy anything with a turkey. Other benefits such as an annual trip as a gift/bonus or a season ski pass are not cash nor cash-equivalents.

HEALTHCARE INSURANCE

This is the behemoth, the biggest, most expensive, and most difficult benefit to negotiate. I'm going to be fairly general about this, because you will want to be very up-to-date on the latest versions of the law.

Some of the provisions of the Affordable Care Act (ACA, also known as Obamacare), or health care law, apply only to larger employers, generally those with more than 50 full-time employees or equivalents. Note: if you have fewer than 50 employees, but are a member of an ownership group with 50 or more full-time equivalent employees, you are subject to the rules for large employers.

If you have 49 or fewer full-time equivalent employees, you can choose to offer insurance through the federal government's SHOP Marketplace or any other source, including your state's marketplace. But the law does not say you *must*, you won't face a penalty if you don't.

You may also offer your employees the ability to buy into group insurance through your company, which they can pay for themselves. Or, you may offer this benefit with you paying a percentage and the employee paying a percentage. I generally recommend that you do pay some percentage of this as a benefit for the team building reasons mentioned above.

If you are self-employed with no employees, you may purchase individual insurance for yourself through your state marketplaces or through the federal marketplace, depending upon your state. Your company can reimburse you if you purchase it, so you can pay for it personally. As a self-employed person, the owner of an S Corp, the owner of a partnership, or the owner of a DBA the insurance is reported as an expense to the company as compensation to the owner (looks like income), then is deducted as Self Employment insurance expense on your personal return.

CAN YOUR COMPANY AFFORD IT?

Obviously, health care insurance is very expensive. You need to make sure that offering it, which is recommended, will not bankrupt your company. It is important to remember that, as in real estate, everything is negotiable at the group policy level.

Deductibles, how much coverage you offer, is all negotiable. You will want, if not need, a good health insurance agent or broker to give you all your options and help you negotiate a benefits package that your company can afford and that will be of help to your employees.

One way to structure benefits so that they are more affordable, is to pay for the employee, and have the employee cover the cost of a spouse and children. Or perhaps you'll offer to cover the employee and spouse. Your agent or broker will be able to help you with the available options.

Other options for your company include offering either a stipend or bonus to cover insurance. Offer your employees a certain amount every month for them to use towards health insurance, and they could choose to accept it or not. A stipend can also be offered for other benefits, such as cell phones or internet, etc. Keep in mind, that a stipend will always be considered taxable income because it could effectively be used for something else.

HEALTHCARE CO-OPS

Another reasonable option for healthcare insurance is health insurance cooperatives. We love ours. We use a Christian co-op called Christian Healthcare Ministries. A health insurance cooperative is a cooperative entity that has the goal of sharing medical expenses by its like-minded members.

Co-ops generally have stipulations to join, such as a faith-based affiliation, but they are usually significantly cheaper than traditional healthcare insurance. They all work slightly different depending on how they set themselves up, so be careful, and do your research. Generally, the members of the co-op pay a monthly fee, and that money is put into an account. As members receive healthcare, the administrative entity of the co-op pays the bills from that account.

A resource for information on this is The Citizen's Counsel for Health Freedom at cchfreedom.org. They have a comparison chart and basic information of most common health share programs.

HEALTHCARE SAVINGS ACCOUNTS

Employers of all sizes may offer a Healthcare Savings Account (HSA) and insurance plans to employees rather than traditional insurance. The premium for a High-Deductible Health Plan (HDHP) is usually less than the premium for traditional health insurance. A higher deductible lowers the premium because the insurance company no longer pays for routine healthcare.

An HSA is a tax-advantaged medical savings account available to taxpayers in the United States who are enrolled in a HDHP. The funds contributed to an account are not subject to federal income tax at the time of deposit. HSA funds roll over and accumulate year to year if not spent.

As of the date of this writing (in 2017), you can save up to $6,750 a year for a family under the age of 50. If someone in your plan is over 50, they can add in an additional $1,000 annually as a Catch-Up plan. That pre-tax money goes into the HSA—we're going back to that tax mentality as a business owner. That money can be used for your deductible, or it can be used for other medical-related things based on IRS guidelines. All deposits to an HSA become the property of the policyholder (employee), regardless of the source of the deposit.

If you have a $10,000 deductible, and you sprain your ankle and you want to make sure it's not broken, you can use the money in the HSA to pay for the x-rays and it remains pre-tax dollars. At no time do you pay tax on that money, unless you use it for a non-medical expense. That's a huge benefit and the amount in the HSA can build up year after year.

HSAs are similar to IRAs in that you may self-direct investments, so you can invest the money to get a better rate of return if you think that it's going to be several years before you need that money. Some financial institutions who offer HSAs also offer investments from "inside" the HSA, but most HSA custodians offer low-risk CDs, stocks, bonds, or mutual funds, so you will get the capital gains, the long-term, short-term capital gains return on investment in those mutual funds. If you choose this keep in mind that as with all investments the money can be "lost" in the market.

The other great thing with an HSA is that some medical expenses not usually covered under most health care policies, such as glasses, dentistry, chiropractic care, or hearing aids, may be purchased using pre-tax funds from your HSA. It can be used for anything medical, even prescription massages.

Remember that withdrawals for non-medical expenses are treated very similarly to those in an IRA, if you don't use the funds for medical expenses, you will be taxed on a withdrawal.

LIFE INSURANCE

When you own a business, especially one with employees, you can get life insurance and make your company (or your employees) the beneficiary. This is an exit strategy (we'll be talking more about exit strategies in the next chapter) where you can take care of your team and the business if something happens to you, their leader.

Think about when a person loses their life and how much of a hole it leaves behind. If your business has employees and you lose your life, how is your company going to continue without you? Will it close its doors? Do the employees take over? If it is a sudden death, how will your employees cope? Even if the business closes, you very well may wish to ease their transition to finding a new job by leaving a type of severance pay for them.

The beauty of Life Insurance is that the payout is tax free. Why? When an individual buys a policy, the premium is typically paid with after tax dollars or with business dollars, so the beneficiaries don't pay any tax on the money.

An insurance agent or broker will be able to help you identify the life insurance that works best for you and your company. It's generally not expensive, unless you have pre-existing medical issues.

We don't typically plan for the end of our life, or even the end of our business's life. We're going to tackle that in the next chapter.

IT'S YOUR TURN

If there were no financial barriers, what kind of benefits would you offer yourself and your team?

_____

_____

_____

_____

What kind of benefit package can your company afford that comes the closest to the ideal package?

_____

_____

_____

_____

Do you need to gradually raise your rates so you can create a better benefits plan for your team and yourself? How much? Will the market support it?

_____

_____

_____

_____

***For FREE Spreadsheets and Forms,
visit RockinYourBusinessFinances.com.***

CHAPTER 10
EXIT STRATEGY

A few years ago, Bob's best friend passed away suddenly in an accident at the age of 52. He left behind a wife and two children. Every single day, Bob's friend made someone feel important. He let his children and his family know he loved them. When he passed, not a single person said he didn't live his life to the fullest.

Bob can't help thinking, "That could have been me. What if I suddenly died like that? What would happen to my wife, my kids, and my team? Would I be as well remembered as my friend or would I leave a mess behind me?"

You want your business to live its life to the fullest too and someday it is going to end. Define your exit strategy because the end will come, it's another given. One of two things will happen, either you end and the business ends with you, or the business is going to transition out of your life, either by selling it or closing it down.

DISABILITY AND END OF LIFE STRATEGY

We talked about life insurance in Chapter 9 and how it can take care of the financial needs of the business in case of your death, but you'll still need to leave detailed instructions to make sure that everything happens as you wish. Sit down and jot down some notes.

How do you want the business to go on in the event of your death or if illness/ injury prevents you from running it?

_____

_____

_____

Who will ensure the customers needs are met?

_____

_____

_____

Who would make decisions for the business?

_____

_____

_____

Who would own the business and how would they run it?

_____

_____

_____

How would the business switch hands?

_____

_____

_____

_____

Who would get all the paperwork done?

_____

_____

_____

How will they find the information they need to run the business the next day?

_____

_____

_____

How is the money from your life insurance to be used?

_____

_____

_____

Once you've answered these questions, and any others that you can think of, get it all into a formal document, and keep it with the appropriate people, your lawyer, CPA, and spouse. If you have a partner, do this planning together. Once you've made the plan, involve all the appropriate professionals to make sure all tax and financial documents are organized to execute the plan.

SELLING YOUR BUSINESS

Some businesses do not lend themselves to being sold. A me, myself and I—aka solo entrepreneur business—is unlikely to be sold. It would probably be closed. Some small businesses, even with a team, are completely dependent on the owner. Other businesses could easily continue with a new management team in place.

For other kinds of businesses, though, selling may be a very viable option. There are people who will be interested in buying your business because they see your success, especially when they see you manage your money, know your numbers, have good margins, and make a profit. They think, "I could just buy that and I could have that same success."

But the reality can look more like this:

> There was a fabulous restaurant in Durango, Colorado. It had been in the same family for generations. Their food was flat out delicious. Everybody loved the place! The owners finally said, "Okay, we're done. None of the kids really want to continue this. We'll sell the business." They sold the building, the Mexican Restaurant, the business name, and walked away. The customers went in for the same experience they'd always had and walked out with something completely different. The restaurant was closed within six months.

Savvy buyers know that the value isn't just in the location and the name, it's in the process and systems. As you're transitioning out of a business, you want your processes in place and you want to be able to explain them to a prospective buyer, especially if there is a buy-out provision in the contract where you receive money later down the road or based on the success of the business. When selling your business, sell it as if you're going to help them be the new boss. It's not just about you making a ton of money. If you've succeeded, it makes sense that when you sell your business that you would want to help encourage the next success. Don't just say, "Hey, give me your money and I'm outta here." You'll be remembered long after you've left as someone who passed on a legacy, instead of just a business.

Your buyers have probably put everything they own in loans or up as collateral to buy a dream, and so the worst thing you can do for your legacy is to just take the money and run. As you're planning your exit strategy, you want to plan training those new people. They can eventually change their systems once they know how you've been successful, but they must keep the business alive first. Remember how the Mexican Restaurant went under right away because they just took their money and ran? Another local restaurant changed hands, virtually the same scenario. They had a turnkey Pizza Parlor and a great business model. The locals loved the recipes and there were many regulars, the owners were ready to move on and a nice, sweet, young couple bought it.

The owner said, "Well, we could just say good luck...but we'll train you on all of our recipes, teach you how we do it, and then as you progress in the business, go ahead and add your own recipes. We recommend that you put them in as specials first. If you've got a new funky little pizza, instead of making a new menu of all new funky pizzas, put your new pizza in as a special and test it out to see if the clients like it or not. If they love it or they're requesting that special again, then you can put that item on the menu."

As a direct result of that scenario, this young couple (with their little kids folding napkins and mom-in-law who runs the front counter) now have a family-owned business that is thriving. They are doing exactly what the exit plan called for, and everybody wins: the former owner bequeathed a legacy, they have a great business, and the customers still have wonderful pizza.

The owner sold them his business with a certain mindset: "We want to transition out. We want this business to stay here for our customers, and we want to give someone else the opportunity to run it and be successful."

YOUR BUYERS ARE YOUR LEGACY

If you really care about your product after you are gone, you will care who you will sell your business to and what they will do with it. We have an electrical wiring system in our home from a family-owned, wonderful, little company that did great work with custom wiring systems. When they decided to sell to another company, they believed that the new owners would continue to support their products so their customers would be taken care of. Shortly after the sale, the new company decided to stop producing and supporting this wiring system, so now anyone with a system from the first company is simply going to have to hope that it won't give out or need repair in the near future, because they will have to completely change their system. Unfortunately, they didn't leave a great legacy for their customers.

ALL IN THE FAMILY

What about selling it to family? What if you were going to transition ownership from you to your kids or you to your brother? When you die, the people that inherit what you have get a basis of what the inheritance is worth when you die.

Let's use real estate as an example. Mrs. Wilson, an independent widow, bought her house back in 1970 for $30,000. The neighborhood has become an exceptionally expensive neighborhood. Although she has made virtually no improvements, it is probably worth $700,000. Let's say she has transferred ownership to her children while she's still alive and they decide to sell it. The children are going to have to pay capital gains on the profit. Since Mrs. Wilson transferred the property prior to her death, the children have the same basis $30,000. If they sell the house for $700,000 then they can deduct the amount they paid to the realtor plus the basis. They'd pay capital gains tax on the remaining profit.

If instead, she dies and leaves the house to them, their basis for the capital gain is the value at the time of her death. If they sell it right away, the capital gain may be nothing. So, if Mrs. Wilson died in 2017 with a home value of $700,000 that value would pass on to the heirs. If they sold the house for $700,000, they would show a loss on the transaction for the realtor fee.

Depending on the value of your company, if you plan on passing it, you need an estate attorney and a CPA to determine the best way to plan for taxes and estate taxes. Estate taxes change so it's very important that you not try to do this yourself. If your company has a large value, the family may feel forced to sell. We see this with a lot of farms. The value of the land far exceeds what the farm produces and the estate taxes are so high the family must sell to pay the taxes. You will want to figure out where you are in that range and adjust accordingly.

A farm is going to be different than a retail business. A partnership is going to be different than an S Corp. This is not the place to go through all those things. You'll want to go over this with your attorney and CPA, have them work as a team for the best results. You will want both, since most attorneys don't know tax code and most CPAs don't know specific property law. Talk things over with your lawyer, your CPA, your business partner, your family, think about it, and then set it up so it works for everyone involved.

EMPLOYEE VESTING STRATEGY

You can sell your company to the employees. I've seen a lot of companies make profit-sharing plans or stock options, and that's also a great way to transition over a longer period. Rather than giving employees a year-end bonus, you might give them shares of the company. This incentivizes the employees. If you have a loss, then they also have a loss. If the company has a gain, you all get a bonus.

You might simply have an understanding (or even a contract) that when/if you sell the company, the employees get first right of refusal. You might tell your employees, "Here's what we believe the sales price will be. If you think you want to buy the business, we need to start setting you up to be in the position to buy the business."

Any time you give benefits to an employee, that's you caring about your team. You're setting them up to win. Believe me, they will notice that and in turn care about the company.

WALKING AWAY WITH HONOR

There's no law that says you can't just lock the doors one night and simply not re-open the next morning. It happens all the time. Employees show up and can't get in. That's when and how they find out they're out of a job, no matter what's going on in their work or personal lives.

This is not a great way to increase your standing in the community. Keeping your team in the loop is difficult at times, but it will be worth it for both their sake and your reputation. You might say, "Let's put a plan in place because this business really isn't doing what we thought it was going to do. It's not making the kind of money we thought it would make. We need an exit strategy for closing the doors." Be honorable and tell your team what's happening. It's a difficult thing to hear, but it's better than no warning.

Even at a time where money is running out, this is a great time to bring in a resume coach to help your team transition on.

An advance of a potential closing is an opportunity to lay off the people that really haven't been good employees anyway. Saying, "We're going to be closing our doors, and we're just downsizing in preparation for that" is acceptable and often necessary. It may also help give you the ability to give a better cushion to your best employees.

It's very important to remember most of the time, even under an LLC or an S Corp, any debts that your business has is going to be held against whatever you own. If you owe vendors, then you must liquidate your assets to pay off those vendors. If you owe the bank, chances are you will personally continue to owe the bank. Try not to put yourself into bankruptcy. If you're already headed in that direction anyway because the debts are so high, then think through selling what you can, get as much money as possible, and pay down those debts before closing the doors.

The key is to not throw away good money after a failing business by taking on more debt. If you're struggling and you're taking on more debt to pay payroll, then this is when you really do need to say, "Okay, we can't do it. We're going to have to lay people off."

YOUR BUSINESS AS AN INVESTMENT

We're nearly at the end of this book but, back at the beginning, we started by thinking about why are we building a business, *this* business, in the first place? Is it because we're professional pizza makers or professional widget makers or professional coaches?

Most businesses are built as an investment. You've put these processes in place, so now it's an investment. An investment is only as good as its sale price or the return from that investment. Out in the world we buy a stock at *this* price and we sell it at *that* price, and the profit or loss is the difference between those two prices.

That's probably where the most value of your business is going to be, in the sales price. Or in the potential returns from the business profit. If you get all your processes in place, the financial processes, the product process and the profit process. Then, eventually you might feel a little like, "Yeah, I'm kind of bored with this. Let me go do something different." Now you have a really good product that you can sell or easily duplicate. Easily replicated processes are, of course, the hallmark of a business that can have multiple locations or become a franchise, and they make it much easier for you to sell.

Essentially, the point of this whole chapter is to plan. Don't let the exit simply happen to you or your business. We want your business to be a blessing to someone, not a curse. How can you make your business endlessly profitable so that it can be your legacy and continue moving forward when you're no longer in the picture? When my dad died, he owned Beeby Enterprises, Inc., and had no will. What happened to Beeby Enterprises, Inc? It just...went away. It went away so completely that I couldn't even have the name. My own family legacy walked out the door because there was no will and no exit strategy. Don't let that happen to you.

IT'S YOUR TURN

Have you decided what you wish to have happen to your business in the case of your death?

_____

_____

_____

_____

_____

_____

_____

What vision do you have as the end goal for your business?

_____

_____

_____

_____

_____

_____

_____

_____

Have you thought about leaving your business to a family member or the entire family? Do you have the transition plans outlined and ready?

_____

_____

_____

_____

_____

_____

_____

_____

Have you thought about how you will transition the business for your employees?

_____

_____

_____

_____

_____

_____

_____

_____

***For FREE Spreadsheets and Forms,
visit RockinYourBusinessFinances.com.***

CHAPTER 11

RECAP

Did you write notes in the book? Go back and look at your notes. Use them as often as you need to in order to build your business. Check out the companion site to this book, RockinYourBusinessFinances.com, for more resources and form templates. If you get all of this down, you can run your business forever. But I haven't taught you how to grow, how to market, how to sell, or how to manage your employees. There's so much more to know, so pace yourself, because it can all be very overwhelming.

Don't stop here. Keep picking up interesting books. Keep reading. Keep looking for more information on how you can perform better in business. I'm a business coach, and I've been overwhelmed lately trying to learn more about social media, blogging, and podcasting. None of us will ever know it all. You won't need some things, but you will need other things.

There are multiple tax laws that benefit small businesses placed by our governments for our advantage—learn them and use them wisely. Small business owners are at the greatest risk of spending the most money on taxes, usually, because we're not paying attention or don't have a good source of information to use all that is available to us. We have the greatest opportunity to take advantage of these things that we're talking about so that our tax liability is super, super low. The problem with small business owners is most have no clue that these exist.

When we hire a CPA to do our taxes, most of us don't ask questions on how to lower our tax liability; we just ask for a tax return. Most CPA's will know how to help you, if you know to ask.

Use the workbook pages in this book—that's where the real work is, applying the knowledge to your particular situation and business. Do the work on finding your benefits, figuring out your cash flow, and doing your budgets. They are great starting points, but they will not be your end points.

As I mentioned, I originally trained under Dave Ramsey. I used his budget form for years and now I use my own. You'll start off by using mine, and years from now you'll probably be using something else, something that works well for your business and your situation.

I hope you've been scribbling in the margins. I hope the pages are tattered. I hope the cover is beat up from being carried from place to place. Share this book with friends, but don't give it away—there's almost no way you'll be able to absorb or do everything in this book all at once. Proficiency will take time, possibly years. You will set everything in motion and you will need to keep coming back, making notes for yourself and keep making adjustments.

I've tried to note which rules and laws will change, but learn them now anyway. Once you've learned them, you'll learn to change with them, because you'll have learned the concepts and fundamentals behind them. Instead of reacting with, "Oh no, it's changed, what am I going to do?" you'll be able to note the change and simply move along.

As you're clipping along in your business, if you start to feel like the financial piece is slipping, you don't have a handle on it, you start to get overwhelmed, or you have a financial decision to make, come back to the book. Come back to the chapters. Keep coming back to the book because the answers are most likely here, or not far off.

You know, one of the best business books I ever read had something I noticed was missing, so I called the writer and said, "I loved your book, but *this* was missing." Now we're good friends, personally and professionally. If you have a question or note that something is missing, or you want to hash something out with me, my contact information is at the end of the chapter.

A book with a whole bunch of tools in it is great, but if you're struggling to apply those tools to your situation, you probably need a coach. Even while writing this book, I know 100% of the time that I can't hit 100% of the people. Your business is different. Everybody's business is different. I can walk into a room full of financial coaches and every single one of them is going to have a different business structure. Every single one has a different niche. Find a coach that works for you. Gather the professionals you need to run a business, not a hobby. You'll need a CPA to help you with your numbers, a lawyer to help you with your legal matters, a financial advisor to help you with your retirement plans, and a coach to talk you through the nitty gritty of your business. Please feel free to call or email me with any questions—and if you need help that I can give you, I'll do it.

Develop your tax mindset. Remember that your business's money is still your money—look for those known advantages, know your disadvantages, and look for those deals.

Here's to running a business sanely.
Here's to endless profitability.
Here's to your success!

Christine Odle
RockinYourBusinessFinances.com

ACKNOWLEDGMENTS

Have you ever read a book that sticks with you for weeks, months, years? That has an impact on your life whether you knew it at the time you were reading it or not?

In 2014, I was invited into Dan Miller's 48 Days Mastermind Group. At the time it was what I would have thought to be way out of my league. I was amazed by all the people who were brought together just because we had followed the idea of *48 Days to The Work You Love*.

One of the members, Emily Chase Smith, had just finished a book that spoke to me— *The Financially Savvy Entrepreneur*. I devoured the book! Emily thought like ME. We had the same vernacular, even though she was a California beach girl and I was a Colorado mountain girl. So, I picked up the phone and called her. It was that simple.

"Emily, I just loved your book! Would you like to write your second book with me? I have started the outline." And that was the beginning of a grand adventure.

Next thing I knew I was flying to California to meet this amazing woman! We traveled together to Nashville for a Mastermind event and became great friends! She traveled to Colorado where we worked on a few projects and then the time came for her to help me write my first book. Emily had just switched gears to become a ghostwriter. She knew me well. I would never sit down to a keyboard to type a book, but I could tell her stories and talk through my chapters and she could put it all together for me.

Without Dan Miller's Mastermind and the amazing people who have been pulled together to work together in business and in life—and without meeting Emily—this book would probably still be stuck in my head somewhere.

Thank you Emily!

The friendships from the Mastermind don't stop there! Another amazing friend— James Woosley of Free Agent Press—stepped in when I needed a designer and help getting this book published. His expertise is over the top, and he brought in his super talented daughter Anna to design the bumblebee artwork! I owe a special thanks to him for stepping me through to the finish line!

Thank you Dan Miller, Deb Ingino, and Andy Traub for creating the Mastermind and changing my life forever!

ABOUT THE AUTHOR

Christine Odle is a financial coach for small business owners. She and her husband live in beautiful Norwood, Colorado, where they own four small businesses—all of which they have run debt free since crawling out from under more than $500,000 in debt in 2009.

Christine works with small business owners and offers financial education and coaching to individuals and families via her company's financial wellness programs. She earned a BA in Business & Mathematics from Fort Lewis College and had a background in Banking and Small Business Financial Management. She is a certified and contracted Dave Ramsey coach and a certified Dan Miller coach.

Christine has a passion for teaching people about personal finance, helping them become and remain debt free, and showing them how to build personal wealth. Through her coaching company, Rockin' Beeby Enterprises, LLC, she works with individuals and families as well as small business owners and corporations. She especially loves the incredible impact that can be made in corporate settings, delivering financial wellness programs that feature live workshops, one-on-one coaching, and online resources.

Learn more at

RockinYourBusinessFinances.com

22718148R00083

Made in the USA
Columbia, SC
03 August 2018